THE STATE OF BUSINESS SCHOOLS

Educational and Moral Imperatives
for Market Leaders

By

Frank J. Cavico
Bahaudin G. Mujtaba
Donovan A. McFarlane

ILEAD Academy, LLC
Davie, Florida. United States of America
www.ileadacademy.com

Frank J. Cavico, Bahaudin G. Mujtaba, and Donovan A. McFarlane, 2010. *The State of Business Schools: Educational and Moral Imperatives for Market Leaders*

Cover Design by: Cagri Tanyar
Cover Photo by: Nova Southeastern University

© ILEAD Academy, LLC (2010)

ISBN-13: 978-1-936237-00-5
ISBN-10: 1-936237-00-8

	Subject Code	Description
1:	EDU032000	Education: Leadership
2:	EDU046000	Education: Professional Development
3:	EDU036000	Education: Organizations & Institutions

Printed in the United States of America by ILEAD Academy, LLC. Davie, Florida.

International

ILEAD ACADEMY
Leadership Education and Associate Development Academy

* Dedication *

This book is dedicated to educators and administrators who often receive little or no praise for all the good work they do. Thanks for making a difference!

Table of Contents

Preface

The authors have been involved in schools of business for many years, serving as academic administrators and faculty members; they have also been involved in many faculty and administrator searches, including two schools of business dean searches. The authors thus have acquired an "education," at times the "hard way," which the authors believe might be beneficial to share with you, the reader, in this reflective book about the nature, role, and functions of business schools in the 21st century, particularly the ethical challenges facing business schools and businesses in general. Presently, the world economy is suffering from an economic recession; and once again attention is being focused on the legal and moral conduct of business for this economic crisis. Business schools too are coming into blame for their role in engendering this economic downturn. The authors, therefore, seek to examine the current state of business schools and in particular to focus on the imperatives – practical as well as moral – that will be indispensable for business schools, business students, and businesses to be successful and sustainable and to create a prosperous and just society.

The critical subject matters of governance, accountability - legal and moral - social responsibility, sustainability, and business and academic leadership will be addressed. Moreover, certain practical, yet very important areas for business schools, such as economic challenges, quality assurance, student recruitment, retention, and diversity, accreditation, faculty research and scholarship, as well as faculty training and development, will be discussed. The authors hope that the issues they raise, the points they make, and the insights that they trust can provide, will be useful to academic administrators and faculty members as well as the larger business community; and also the authors sincerely hope that the book will prove instrumental in producing thoughtful, thought-provoking, and stimulating intellectual debate on these important issues facing business schools and businesses.

This is an exceptionally challenging time for business schools and businesses. Seminal and extraordinary changes in business and the economy are occurring, expectations regarding the role of business organizations are evolving, and these changes and expectations must be reflected in schools of business. This is a most challenging environment for business schools, yet it is an exciting time too. This book provides thoughts and "reflections" on several academic areas involving business schools. The authors discuss the challenges confronting business schools, particularly in this very difficult economic climate, while noting some of the opportunities available to schools. The authors discuss the key issue of accreditation, providing some thoughts on the benefits and costs of seeking accreditation (or reaccreditation), and particularly focusing on accreditation by the Association to Advance Collegiate Schools of Business (AACSB).

Closely related to accreditation, of course, is the subject of faculty research and scholarship, and thus the authors supply some thoughts and furnish certain recommendations as to the degree, scope, and quality of such scholarship. The authors deal with the ever-present "balancing act" many schools, especially tuition-driven schools, face, that is, the need to balance student "numbers" with quality. The authors discuss the related topics of student recruitment, retention, and diversity, and also discuss the important subjects of governance and leadership in schools of business, focusing on the critical role of the dean as a formally designated leader of the school. Ethics is examined from three perspectives: 1) the relationship between ethics and leadership; 2) the role of business ethics at a school of business and for businesses generally; and 3) an example and explication of a business ethics course designed for a school's MBA program.

Today's publications and projections in most articles imply that if we are waiting for the economic conditions to return to normal in the business sector, then perhaps we are in for somewhat of a surprise or even a shock, since future leaders will require new skills that are tailored to a continuously changing environment that requires crisis management, urgency in decision-making, and the ability to work with uncertainty. Academic leaders and administrators must make sure that thoughts regarding the possible "shock" of an "uncertain" work environment are reflected upon, discussed with students, and considered for research purposes as well as for the development of new competencies, courses, and perhaps different programs to better prepare their graduates. The "uncertain" prospective workplace might require the integration of "laboratory" activities, such as "shadowing" a manager for a period of time, where students can practice their decision-making skills in dealing with urgent and uncertain outcomes so their business degree can lead to a "sustainable" competitive advantage for their organizations.

The authors underscore what they believe to be the moral imperative of business schools and business. The authors further examine the important and related concepts of social responsibility and governance in the business and business school context, and emphasize the key role of schools of business in inculcating these critical concepts. The authors, finally, provide certain practical advice and recommendations in the area of training and development of faculty, particularly in the area of online programs.

Chapter 1

Business Schools in the 21st Century

Business schools and business education prepare students to learn
the basics of thinking critically, communicating effectively, and
managing small and large enterprises so they can serve society in a
successful manner. Business graduates have become a target for many
critics as they link the ethical lapses of senior executives to major
scandals that have partially led to the financial challenges that the
world is facing today. The questions and thoughts reflected upon in this
book are focused on business schools, business education, faculty
members' qualifications, and the integration of ethical thinking in
business curriculums. The authors offer reflections, suggestions, and
practical "tips" for the consideration of university and college
administrators and business school faculty members.

Introduction

Business schools and business students compete with people from
across the globe with diverse cultural orientations. Critics claim that
business schools focus too much on the achievement of the "bottom-
line" at all costs, and that this indoctrination has led to unethical
behaviors and scandals associated with Enron, Tyco, WorldCom, and
other such firms (Mitroff, 2004; Ghoshal, 2005), as well as the recent
real estate, mortgage, and banking scandal. According to Neubaum,
Pagell, Drexler, McKee-Ryan, and Larson (2009), "many of the recent
discussions of business schools have centered not on the good their
graduates do, but on how the theoretical foundations of business school
education may be linked to ethical lapses and scandals involving
managers who have been subjected to business school training" (p. 9).

The critics argue that business school faculty members teach such concepts as transaction-based economics, economic liberalism, or agency theory to students, which focus on short-term profits, even if this objective comes at a cost of damaging long-term opportunities and relationships with customers, suppliers, and/or vendors (Mitroff, 2004, p. 185). Ghoshal states that "business schools have actively freed their students from any sense of moral responsibility" because faculty members teach theories that are ideological in nature (2005, p. 76).

According to Bennis and O'Toole (2005), business schools are facing heavy criticism for failing to impart useful skills and knowledge, prepare leaders for doing what is right, instill norms of ethical behavior that would have prevented major corporate debacles, and even failing to lead graduates to corporate jobs that can pay them good wages. The root cause of these problems is management education, according to Warren G. Bennis and James O'Toole (2005), in that most business schools seem to have adopted a self-defeating model for assessment of academic excellence. Instead of measuring the quality of each program in terms of the competence of students, most schools assess themselves based on the rigor of scientific research that is published by their faculty and graduates. This model might be appropriate in dentistry, medicine, or chemistry, but perhaps not for business schools. Business schools should use a practitioner-oriented model. However, as mentioned by Bennis and O'Toole, the reality is that most business schools continue to hire and promote research-oriented professors who have never spent time working in the workplace. Since these research-focused faculty members are comfortable teaching methodology and scientific research, business schools will continue to produce graduates of the same caliber. To become competitive and relevant for the modern workplace, Bennis and O'Toole emphasize that business schools need to rediscover the practice of business while effectively balancing the need for educating practitioners and creating knowledge through scientific research.

According to Jacobs, during this "tough" economy, "fingers are increasingly being pointed at the academic institutions that educated those who got us into this mess" (2009, p. A13). Jacobs discussed three failures of sound business practices, which he says lie at the root of the economic crisis; and these failures have not been adequately addressed by business schools: misaligned incentive programs (incentive systems that rewarded short-term gain took precedence over those designed for long-term value creation), understanding the responsibility and obligation of corporate boards, and having an apparent, transparent, and enforceable system of accountability. It is disappointing to see business graduates paying high prices to complete their degrees and yet never hearing lectures on the responsibilities of board members, proper incentive programs, and how to effectively grant and exercise shareholders' rights in modern firms. Jacob says:

> General Electric was stripped of its coveted AAA-rating because of problems emanating from its financial services unit. Yet its board has only one director with experience in a financial institution. If it is the board's job to oversee a corporation, it seems logical that there would be a segment in the core curriculum of every business school devoted to board structure, composition and processes. But most programs don't cover the topic (2009, A13).

If faculty members are failing to teach the principles of corporate governance in the MBA curriculum, then business schools have failed their graduates. Jacob says that "by not internalizing sound principles of governance and accountability, B-school graduates have matured into executives and investment bankers who have failed American workers and retirees who have witnessed their jobs and savings vanish" (2009, A13). Most MBA curriculums require an ethics or law course as part of the program, but this may not be sufficient to deter wrongdoing. Would a person like Ken Lay or Bernie Madoff have acted differently if they had done really well in their ethics and law courses in the business program? Jacob recommends that today's workplace needs a generation of business leaders and graduates who are trained in corporate board responsibilities, accountability for transparent investments, and who are experts in designing compensation systems that promote long-term value for the company and all of its stakeholders. Therefore, "America's business schools need to rethink what we are teaching -- and not teaching -- the next generation of leaders" Jacobs, 2009, A13).

While business school curricula do teach scientific research, efficiency, accuracy, operations management, and economic theories, they also teach students about value creation by maintaining a healthy relationship with their suppliers, colleagues, unions, government entities, and communities for the long-term sustainability of their success. This dichotomy would suggest that studies are needed to see if business schools are in fact driven more toward revenues and profits, or if they are more focused on the long-term success of their graduates. The culture of each school heavily influences what the faculty and staff actually focus on. And the institutional culture of each school is heavily influenced by their top leaders, including the dean, department chairs, and program level directors. As such, it becomes imperative that academics focus on the state of business schools, education, and ethics, since all graduates will eventually end up in the workplace where they will face a challenging and competitive work environment.

The Business School in the 21st Century: A Modular Perspective

Business schools in the 21st century confront daunting challenges relative to their program structures, roles, and functions, particularly how their perspectives shape their success and performance as market leaders (market-drivers) and market followers (market-driven) organizations. Business schools are a vital part of society's quest to understand and develop strategies for survival while dealing with constraints imposed by scarcity and the "change process." There is a great need for more innovation and creativity in business schools nationally and globally, as people experience and live through macro-environmental changes that continually affect one's ability to engage in buying and selling exchanges, leadership, and negotiations across a complex platform of organizations that are local, national, regional, and international. Business schools, therefore, need to develop effective models for the 21st century and beyond; models that will result in success for schools and graduates, organizations, and society. Organizations today are functioning in a highly complex environment where the demand for expertise in several areas is a constantly increasing reality. Accordingly, society needs wiser and better graduates and leaders who can immediately generate direct and measurable value for their organizations; and this objective will not be possible without good business schools with "solid" programs that reflect present and future needs of individuals and society. Moreover, change must be taught, particularly the strategies for effectively managing change through proper knowledge management and project management; and concomitantly planning protocols must be important aspects of the renewed vigor toward developing entrepreneurial leaders, who can effectively respond to today's problems and challenges, and thereby guide society into a prosperous future where growth and sustainability are realistic and attainable. Business schools thus must strive to be leaders and pioneers of economic survival and managerial and business success.

Background and Overview

In the global economy of the 21st century, business schools have been, and are, a major force both as globalizing influences and trend-setters in value and industry practices. Annually, thousands of professors and corporate experts of various branches of business develop and promote new ideas and build upon old models to contribute to a fuller and more progressive understanding of the nature of business, management, leadership, operations, finance, and administration in the global market, where changes in technology, consumer needs and wants, social, cultural, and political values affect the ways in which business is conducted on multiple interconnected platforms. With thousands of schools and colleges of business located around the globe, the number of degrees being conferred in business and related fields is unprecedented. The MBA (Master of Business Administration) degree has become a common qualification among those seeking to enter the global corporate economy as entrepreneurs and advanced professional, managerial, and administrative workers. Actually, the MBA degree itself became a propelling factor in the growth and development of 21st century business schools, establishing a standard platform from which to develop business curriculum, especially at the graduate level. Other degrees such as the MIB (Master in International Business) and MIBA (Master in International Business Administration) which are specialist masters/graduate degrees, along with the MAC (Masters in Accounting), have been instrumental in affecting the pedagogical processes of business schools across the globe. The MBA as a generalist degree has in many instances given way to emerging, yet not quite as popular "soft" graduate business degrees, such as the MSM (Master of Science in Management), Master of Science in Human Resources Management (MSHRM), Master of

Science (MS) in specialties such as Leadership, Organizational Leadership, Project Management, and Retail Management. Regardless of a definite need to develop beyond the "MBA cult," business schools and colleges are still conferring this degree in higher numbers than others, as the inherent value and perceived prestige remain constant in the fervent minds of men and women with strong inclinations and high aspirations toward corporate and entrepreneurial endeavors.

The number of business schools and colleges that have emerged in the 21st century is overwhelming; and the advent of online degree programs has created an even larger market for the business degree, especially with the affinity that capitalism holds for fostering independence through wealth creation and the value of formalized business knowledge in resource ventures. Furthermore, business degrees have become more appealing with the opening of new markets in certain geographic regions and the increasing "commodization" and marketization of their cultural and economic practices within a definably interactive global marketspace. For example, Asia and the Middle East, and the countries of China and India, have significantly impacted the growth of business enterprise activities and the global market. Given the growth rates and potential for future business opportunities, business schools and colleges have an extensive global platform on which to construct curriculum, offer training, and build talents. Business degrees are thus extremely popular; and this popularity will not dwindle despite the current slowdown in world and national economies.

According to the U.S. Department of Education, National Center for Education Statistics (2009), of the 1,524,000 bachelor's degrees conferred in 2006–07, the largest numbers of degrees were conferred in the fields of business (328,000). This number is twice the numbers conferred in social sciences and history (164,000), more than three times those conferred in education (106,000), and health sciences (102,000). At the masters' level, the number of business degrees (150, 000) conferred in 2006-07 was only second to that of the education field (177,000) (U.S. Department of Education, National Center for Education Statistics, 2009). As such, business schools and colleges are instrumental in higher education, economic and social progress, and in defining the overall trends in professional development, training, and skills. Given the trend and the instrumental role played by business colleges and schools, they need to constantly build and modify the platforms they use for training and educating the business leaders of today and tomorrow, especially since change and uncertainty collaborate to alter and create new threats and opportunities in the macro-environment. Consequently, the academic and business community need to understand the challenges and problems business schools and colleges face now and in the future; and they must be particularly cognizant of the need for innovation and strategic configuration in curricular practices and "real-world" considerations. Figure 1 graphs the number of degrees at the bachelors' level conferred by fields for three academic years in a 12 year period from 1996.

Figure 1: Trends in bachelor's degrees: 1996–97 and 2006–07

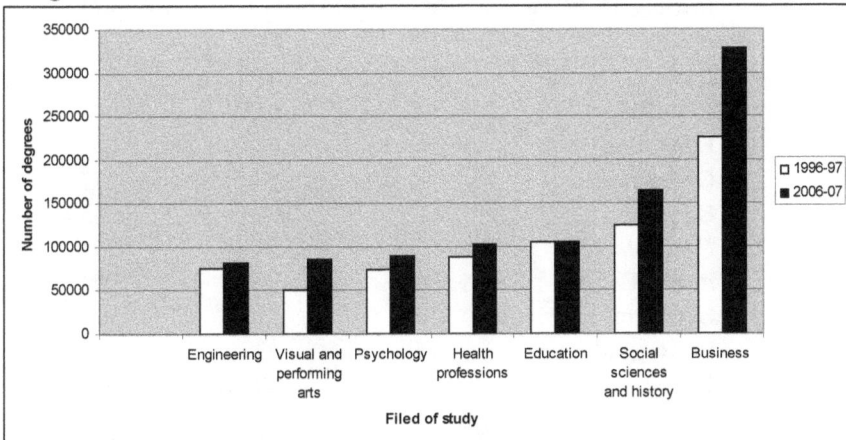

SOURCE: U.S. Department of Education, National Center for Education Statistics, 1996–97, 2001–02, and 2006–07 Integrated Postsecondary Education Data System, "Completions Survey" (IPEDS-C:96–97), and Fall 2001 and Fall 2007.

In Figure 1, the NCES provides a summary of the data: "Of the 1,524,000 bachelor's degrees conferred in 2006–07, the *largest numbers of degrees were conferred in the fields of business (328,000)*, social sciences and history (164,000), education (106,000), and health sciences (102,000). At the master's degree level, the largest numbers of degrees were in the fields of education (177,000) and business (150,000). The fields with the largest number of degrees at the doctor's degree level were health professions and related clinical sciences (8,400), education (8,300), engineering (8,100), biological and biomedical sciences (6,400), psychology (5,200), and physical sciences (4,800)" (NCES, 2009, p. 1). Data demonstrates that the undergraduate business degrees have dominated the period covered by the data, and this dominance continues with this growth trend over the 12-year period in the recent past.

Figure 2: Degrees Conferred by School in Academic Year 2007- 2008, Harvard University.

	Male	Female	Total
College	857	866	1,723
GSAS	554	428	982
Business	600	312	912
Dental	53	46	99
Design	134	102	236
Divinity	81	92	173
Education	143	464	607
Government	340	237	577
Law	421	345	766
Medical	97	99	196
Public Health	185	269	454
Extension			
Undergraduate	55	63	118
Graduate	198	198	396
Total	3,718	3,521	7,239

Source: Registrar's Office, *Harvard University*, 2009.

The national trend in degree conferral by dominant type with business degrees being the greatest in numbers holds for many institutions as well. An examination of Harvard University's degrees conferred by schools and fields-programs in academic year 2007-08 shows that business degrees are at number one spot by program type as seen in Figure 2.

One can observe in Figure 2 that Harvard University Business College conferred more degrees than all other schools except the combined Graduate School of Arts and Sciences. Thus, individually, the College of Business conferred the highest number of degrees in academic year 2007-08. An examination of the number of degrees conferred by program in academic year 2007-2008 also reveals that among 43 different degree types and levels conferred by Harvard University in the fields of sciences and arts, design, divinity, education, government, law, medicine, and public health, there was a total of 907 M.B.A. degrees conferred with 579 conferred on males and 310 on females. The second highest category of degrees conferred by program in same academic year was 588 in law (J.D. degrees). Thus, business degrees are a dominant feature of successful education and educational institutions and programs; and business schools are a major producer of human factors relevant for propelling social and economic systems.

Questions for Business Schools

Given the above relevant understanding supported by statistical trends in education degree conferral by schools and programs, there are several questions one must consider when it comes to the prominent roles that business schools play in 21st century society and education, specifically higher education, in relation to the dynamics and nature of change in the global business environment. The first question which is brought to mind is: Are business schools effectively meeting the real needs or demands of today's complex, global, business environment through curriculum structures and programs? The second question: What are the current and future problems and challenges facing schools of business, and are they effectively responding to them? The third question: Is there a need for greater innovation and creativity in business schools regarding program curriculum and training? The fourth question is: How do business schools prepare for the future, which is surely rapidly evolving, yet an uncertain one? The fifth and final question is: What is a proposed effective model for the 21st century business school? These questions are extremely important, and will serve as guides in exploring the nature, processes, and problems and challenges of business schools in the 21st century, and in examining the change leadership needed in the emerging global business environment, where multiple interconnected factors are changing the world and the terms of economic survival.

1. *Are business schools effectively meeting the real needs and demands of today's complex global business environment through curriculum structures and programs?*

Business schools are expected to be unique sources for pioneering ideas and practices within the current global, complex, rapidly changing, environment where individuals, groups, and institutions - private and public, political and economic - engage in several important activities significant for societal survival. This function requires both innovation and adaptation; and the 21st century's economic and global climate calls for business schools that are able to perform environmental analyses to understand the threats and opportunities available, and to devise effective strategic responses to current and emerging needs and wants of individuals, groups, industries, and societies. Providing effective training that will meet these needs and wants, while responding to problems and challenges in today's global contexts, requires 21st century business schools to develop sound curricular, structural platforms, and programs for training and educating business professionals and practitioners, who are able to increase productivity and to respond to changes in technology, organizational needs, and broader social needs.

In today's global and technologically infused society there is an excess demand for skilled knowledge workers. The knowledge worker is a product of education, technological marvel, and modern development in organizational practices and theories (McFarlane, 2008); and this is the task of business schools in the 21st century – to produce highly skilled knowledge workers who are able to adapt to the changing nature of the macro-environment, business needs, individual and societal needs, and who are able to produce more through skills they have acquired from creative learning systems. In the 21st century, there are thousands of business schools; and business degrees are among the most popular being conferred worldwide. Reports and figures from the National Center for Education Statistics have adequately demonstrated that 21st century business schools are indeed "making the numbers" in terms of graduate professionals and degrees. However, the extent to which they are truly effectively responding to the critical needs of the concurrent and emerging globally complex environment is not quite clear, especially when one considers the myriad problems and challenges being faced by individuals and organizations. Leadership problems are rampant across organizations, and many inept and/or unethical managers and entrepreneurs plague the business world in small and large settings. The recent "flood" of corporate and financial irresponsibility and immorality in the United States of America is demonstrative that "something is lacking" in the educational workings of business professionals and entrepreneurs.

Business schools in the 21st century are offering similar programs and have similar program structures, which make many degrees and degree programs replications of others, as colleges and universities build upon common models being used by "popular" and larger schools and programs. This has created a situation where every MBA appears as just another MBA, or where every business degree appears as just another business degree. Only very few schools have taken an initiative to make their programs unique and innovative by creatively matching design and program structure and contents with concurrent and emerging needs of organizations and society. There appears to be a decisively reactive approach toward replicating or benchmarking what individual schools and business departments use as prototypes of "best" business degrees on the education and economic markets. Yet business schools need to be more creative, environmentally intelligent, and responsive in designing effective and sensible programs that arm individuals with the true knowledge and skills they need to survive and to prosper in a changing and unpredictable global environment. This requires them to invest more rigorously in an intelligence-approach to program design, wherein they teach responsiveness on all levels by fostering solutions-based courses from a dynamic array of potential "real-world" scenarios. Business schools in the 21st century have not done the best job of training and educating their students or graduates to offer more creative and innovative energies in propelling organizations to more efficient and sustainable performance levels and success.

2.   What are the current and future problems and challenges facing schools of business, and are they effectively responding to them?

Twenty-first century business schools are facing several major current problems that prevent them from effectively examining their platforms and structures so as to develop and design more effective and responsive programs. These major current problems stem from the market demand for training and for expert business professionals, declining levels in general academic standards, the dominant role of technology in education, the rapid pace of change, as well as the need to respond with "rushed" supplies of entrepreneurs, corporate workers, skilled employees, extreme competition, high costs of accreditation and promotion, budgetary and agency constraints, and lack of effective leadership at both institutional and business school levels. Competition is one of the major problems faced by business schools as they compete among themselves as well as with non-business schools and institutions that still offer courses and programs in business. These non-specialist business institutions are often able to offer a unique education and diversity of individuals that make them very appealing to even the most demanding of business majors. Competition among business schools has been, and is, a major problem facing individual business schools and programs confronted with promotional strategies and the costs associated with maintaining competitive edge or competitive enrollment. This challenge often requires heavy investment in expensive processes, such as accreditation, costly advertising, and marketing programs, as well as the development of broad corporate networks for funding and reputation-building.

In the future, the number of business schools might decline due to saturation in program types and contents. Unless business schools become more innovative, many will fade away as new needs and markets emerge with demands for more responsive business professionals and more "applied" degree knowledge and skills. Certain business schools today will potentially fail due to inability to maintain their competitive edge, become innovative, and transform their platforms and visions, as the nature and need of the market changes with globalization and new problems and challenges that will emerge from cultural, social, economic, political, and technological changes. Furthermore, the transition of the human race, depending on the current broad-based and global policies and political leadership, could alter the terrain for business opportunities by declining or further integrating the contexts and parameters in which survival and progress will take place. Business schools, accordingly, must recognize themselves as transitional institutions that are responsible for paving the way to economic future and survival for individuals, groups, institutions, and society.

Nonetheless, today's business schools overall are not effectively responding to these problems and challenges because of a culture of "followership" in which schools replicate each others' strategic moves, structures, and programs, rather than earnestly thinking and designing new means and ways of meeting the needs of current and emerging global markets. Business schools are constantly engaged in competitive struggles with each other, and therefore many spend much time in maintaining their status quo so that they can remain viable in very competitive markets. Many of these schools lack the leadership and creativity required to stand out and become pioneers in a new vision for the leadership of business and business schools and programs. Some business schools seem to have reached their maturity in terms of theoretical constructs and development in program platforms and offerings. Nevertheless, this is not absolutely true; rather, what one sees with 21st century business schools is an inability to synthesize "knowledge stocks" to effectively develop degree programs that mirror the transitional nature of organizations and society, where change dictates the next strategic response readily available in the graduates' minds. As a result, the 21st century business schools need to become innovative market-drivers and leaders.

3. Is there a need for greater innovation and creativity in business schools regarding program curriculum and training?

This question closely relates to those above, and was partially answered when the authors explored the changing contexts in which business schools operate. There is without any doubt a need for greater innovation and creativity in business schools regarding program curriculum and training. Business schools need to stop employing philosophical and structural replication as program development methods. and must, like the unique individuals they train and educate, seek to develop extremely distinct competencies which set them apart from their competitors. The 21st century has produced a wealth of knowledge and access to vast amount of resources and information on a global level that should act as a "frontier" for innovative and strategic vision, endeavors, and programs. Business schools thus must recognize that there is no limit on their abilities to develop new rules and theories regarding the globalized business context in which individuals and organizations operate. They must develop a more "holistic" view of the field of business by seeking to integrate business and other knowledge fields to create curricula and programs.

Innovation is needed to change the approaches business schools take in educating and training their pupils. Business schools in the 21st century base their platforms on past corporate models of success that may lack efficiency and effectiveness where competition narrows the opportunities available for their graduates. While they emphasize practical aspects of business education in theoretical or hypothetical presentations, they fail to accurately replicate or mirror true-life contexts that impact individual and organizational success. The need for more realistic understanding and conceptions of the "real-world," as well as what is required of new entrant-entrepreneurs or business professionals, must be more effectively simulated in business programs to avoid a new wave of ineffective and unethical business leaders and consequently business failures that become the trigger for broad corporate immorality and social irresponsibility.

There is, therefore, a greater need for planning by business schools, especially in the areas of project management and knowledge management as foundational platforms upon which to develop the new or next popular business degree, particularly since the MBA, which has been a hallmark achievement of the business school, may not be or remain as appealing or valued as it was in previous decades. Many business schools have built programs on the original MBA platform and then have offered programs such as MIB (Master in International Business) MIBA (Master in International Business Administration), and EMBA (Executive MBA), along with business degrees in related fields such as management, for example the Master of Science in Management (MSM), as well as a variety of other degrees – "hard" and "soft" - in business at both graduate and undergraduate levels.

However, most of these programs may not be innovative enough in terms of their structures and contents, especially when it comes to mirroring the actual knowledge and skills platform required in a globally diverse environment, where divergent and convergent thinking processes are integrated into the complex of political and economic life. Business schools, therefore, need to become examples as well as exemplars of the creativity and innovation they seek to foster in their students.

4. How do business schools prepare for the future, which is surely a rapidly evolving, yet uncertain, one?

Given the above understanding, business schools plainly face a challenge in preparing for a future where 21st century changes and problems will emerge. This will be a future in which the struggle for both individual and organizational survival becomes more hard-pressed by declining resources and a "tighter" world market, in which more reality-based curricula and programs will be needed to effectively train individuals to survive and to ascertain and take advantage of opportunities in the fierce "human jungle." Complicated by the need to recognize the intimate relationship between people and environment, and the attendant collective consumption effects, business schools will need to become more concerned about interrelationships existing among societal sectors and fields of study to effectively respond to emerging needs of individuals and organizations. When one examines current economic crises, and thereby recognizes how such occurrences can change the world and survival therein, one realizes that business schools need to position themselves to be institutes that are able to foster and promote a variety of alternatives regarding how to survive and to prosper. "Economization" needs to be reconsidered as part of a bedrock philosophy of business undertakings from a strategic perspective tied in to change management, leadership, and knowledge management practices that are applicable across contexts and continents.

In the 21st century, business schools must teach change and educate their students on the nature of present and evolving business environment by using effective cases and examples to "bridge the gap" between the theoretical and practical. This objective requires having a broader philosophical platform that allows for knowledge integration in the form of a "holism" that develops entrepreneurs and corporate professionals who are more well-rounded and, hence, more flexible and adaptive when it comes to the application or use of knowledge, inquiry, communication, creativity, and problem-solving skills. Graduates of future business schools must be educated as not only change-agents and managers, but also as creative adapters, who are able to alter their thinking and tailor solutions to respond to whatever business problems and challenges may arise. Educating today's graduates to be tomorrow's corporate leaders and entrepreneurs requires 21st century business schools to develop an attitude built on the ideas of ethics, sustainability, and "posterity preservation" amidst looming economic crises, which, if trends analyses prove correct, will be significant in altering the opportunities available for entrepreneurial pursuits and economic survival in future global and local markets.

Many of the programs in 21st century business schools are structured with contents or courses that dwell largely on famous and very successful entrepreneurial figures and extremely well-publicized and wealthy organizations. This pattern might need to change to better prepare business graduates and professionals for the current and emerging reality of business, as the academic community attempts to see where competitive forces, especially those associated with world population change and technology and job transfers, are modifying the "playing field" or landscape of business. Business schools thus need to teach individuals how to survive by stressing creativity and craft entrepreneurship as viable and equally important tools in becoming successful. So many individuals leave business schools with images of corporate "tycoons" etched in their minds, and consequently unrealistically position themselves with fantasy aspirations that are very hard to come by, particularly in the present and near future business environments. Business schools should now teach "reality," and thereby emphasize the personal growth aspect of business degrees as viable "ports" for improving individual life, survival, and prosperity through creative thinking processes and presenting a "true" picture of the "real-world."

5. What is a proposed effective model for the 21st century business school?

In recognizing the problems and challenges confronted by business schools in the 21st century, and in consideration of the future of business schools and business education, there clearly is a need for more effective and strategically sound program models and structures to respond to present and emerging needs as individuals, groups, institutions, and a society. Business schools must recognize their roles in creating and affecting current and future economic pathways through their teaching and training of today's and tomorrow's business leaders. Developing an effective model or platform for sound business education requires business schools to understand the current and future environments in which they operate, and will operate, and in which their students and graduates must live and survive economically.

Recognizing the continuous tendency toward cultural, social, economic, and political integration, as well as technological interconnectedness and continued globalization of economies and markets, a Global Trends model and approach would be an ideal beginning platform for developing effective business school models in current and future contexts. This approach will allow business schools to develop and administer flexible programs and curricula as they strive to match, respond to, as well as to develop, strategic modules that attempt to replicate and model "real-world" scenarios in present and emerging contexts. Global Trends analysis allows for business schools to decisively provide broad-based knowledge for their students thereby matching all vital sectors of the macro-environment, which consequentially fosters a globalized and change-ready and adaptive perspective. Such a model effectively utilizes a knowledge management and applications approach to learning that enhances individuals' understanding of the critical need for fostering a dynamic perspective in dealing with business problems and challenges.

In the 21st century, business schools depend highly on technology to accomplish their missions. With this in mind, the need to integrate relevant technology education in business school programs and curriculum cannot be overlooked, especially in the era of the knowledge worker. Appropriately using knowledge systems in determining learning methods, strategies, program contents, and program-critical mission is essential. "Knowledge systems are the core requirements for organizing, controlling, and collaborating across systems of people, structures, and processes (organizational system, structure, & process knowledge – OSSPK) in order to develop organizational capability through establishing and having grasp of valuable project management body of knowledge (PMBOK), while determining the type of leadership and managerial knowledge (LMK) required to effectively guide the organization, accomplish its mission and goals, while meeting macroenvironmental and microenvironmental challenges to secure opportunities for growth, survival, competitive advantage, and market leadership" (McFarlane, 2008, p. 1). As a result, the 21st century business schools must understand this interconnected medium within which they function if they are to effectively reach their goals and graduate capable business professionals and entrepreneurs, who are not only versed in strategic thinking, but also in managing knowledge to increase their individual and organizational performance and success - now and in the future.

The Homogenous Model
   The rapidly changing business environment of the 21st century has given rise to the demand for well-rounded business professionals and experts who are able to work and lead organizations through economically and politically turbulent times. This demand cries out for a solid educational foundation in business principles and practices backed by the ability to be flexible and adaptive to circumstances brought on by the change and the uncertainty. Business schools in the 21st century, therefore, must ensure that their programs are designed to offer the individual the relevant skills and knowledge needed to survive change, and in addition, to respond effectively to the current problems and challenges, and to strategically prepare for whatever the future holds. There is a need to recognize the role that effective program models play in preparing entrepreneurs, scholars, and business professionals to deal with the theoretical and practical aspects of business operations, inventions, and forecasts. Business schools must understand the trends that characterize global markets and that shape the contexts of success, especially regarding opportunities and growth in a competitive climate, where resource constraints minimize the

avenues through which people accomplish individual and organizational goals.

The educational foundations of business schools must be firmly rooted in the contexts of change and survival economics and use a holistic approach towards understanding and responding to the SWOTs (Strengths, Weaknesses, Opportunities, and Threats) that are faced in the quest to optimize resource consumption and utilization, while concomitantly promoting and ensuring sustainable and ethical development for posterity in a highly competitive globalized marketplace and market-space. Business schools of the 21st century must become a part of understanding and fostering the advocated interconnection between an individual and his or her environment in order to better teach the art as well as science of balanced production, exchange, consumption, and conservation as vital to a continued economic progress.

Yet there appears to be a lack of uniqueness among the majority of 21st century business schools and their programs. This situation may stem from a lack of innovation and creativity by curriculum specialists, leaders, and administrators of business schools, as well as many professors and instructors. In fact, regrettably, the same lack of innovation and creativity can be passed on to many graduates who are unable to be successful managers, strategists, and entrepreneurs in the workplace. While some business schools have tried to distinguish themselves by attempting innovation in program design and structure, training, and the education of their students, by far the majority of business schools seem to just be replicas of previously successful ones; and many "regular-rated" business schools "merely" seek to emulate Ivy League schools or other well-known "prestige" programs in developing and designing their own curricula.

When one examines "mainstream" academia in comparison to "alternative" academia, that is, meaning educational pursuits offering studies in subjects and disciplines that have been excluded from "regular" universities and colleges because of the quest for capitalism and competitive industries, one realizes that these alternative schools may be more innovative and creative in their program contents and offerings because they lack both the pressure to conform and be a part of a specific body of policies or politics that confines education and personal development. In the United States, business schools generally seek and possess accreditation under general charters of regional accreditation bodies – that is, "umbrella" accreditation, but there are three specialized agencies that provide specific business program or business school accreditation in the United States and elsewhere. They are the AACSB (Association to Advance Collegiate Schools of Business), IACBE (International Assembly for Collegiate Business Education), and ACBSP (Association of Collegiate Business Schools and Programs), with the two former appearing as the most prominent, and the AACSB being in more demand nationally. This poses a problem as schools of business compete on accreditation types despite program structures and contents, which in many cases might be homogenous and even inferior in schools where one type of the three business accreditations above might be perceived as superior. For example, there seems to be certain perceptions among many schools and colleges of business that AACSB is superior to the others, and this view leads to resistance for faculty and students holding accredited business degrees from schools certified by IACBE and ACBSP as well as regionally accrediting bodies. This situation poses a challenge for business schools and colleges despite the replication of business programs by credit and course structures.

Many business schools and colleges, especially those that are "young" in the market, tend to develop their program structures and contents based on models and curricula being used by already established and successful schools. However, who is to say that the models and programs structures and content being used by such schools are better or even the best in the "industry." It is similar to the brand effect present between Ivy League and "regular" schools regarding degree, educational value, and instructions, among other quality indicators. Business accreditation does not determine how creative a school is or how innovative its training and education are in preparing individuals for success in the corporate world and the global marketplace. The jobs of faculty, staff, and educational leaders are to secure the relevant accreditation for the schools and distinguish themselves through innovation as well as unique and value-creating curricula.

Market Leaders and Followers

Business schools in the 21st century, similar to other institutional units or organizations, can be assessed based on their profiles regarding their positions in terms of innovativeness, creativity, market-orientation, brand image, inventiveness, quest toward services diversification, vision, core and distinct competencies, competitive advantages, and leadership; that is, key facts are whether they are market leaders or merely followers; and certainly some do lead in the business training and education market while others simply follow. Business schools that are leaders are those with a unique and advanced understanding of the macro-environment and intricacies of the marketplace, a well-formulated mission and vision statement, a quest to make a significant difference in individual and organizational contexts, a talent for new ideas, highly skilled thinkers and facilitators, effective project management and planning orientation, knowledge management approach toward "packaging" training, technological know-how, and the ability and technical facilities and faculty to empower a new generation of entrepreneurially-savvy thinkers to deal with current and future challenges on individual and organizational levels.

The majority of academic organizations are merely "followers," and the same "distinction" holds for business schools and colleges. Many business schools and colleges observe their competitors as well as follow the examples of the market's most successful ones in designing and developing their programs, their strategies, and in the way they educate and relate to their pupils. Business schools and colleges that are followers in the market lack the innovativeness and creativity needed to place them at the head of the competitive game; therefore, they are active observers and imitators in a highly competitive education market. Yet despite being followers, they are often highly successful because they are able to capitalize on costs savings associated with dependence on secondary data source and established, prior knowledge and ideas that have been proven by the market leaders.

Followers are generally those business schools and business colleges that are afraid to take risks; and hence they only anticipate the actions of their competitors, rather than taking initiatives to be first-movers in some new ideas, projects, or inventions. Business schools in the 21st century face so many challenges and problems in the mature competitive school market that they are often reluctant to change what is already in their "views" a successful strategy, program, or program structure. However, the rate of change is so rapid that innovation and adaptation require change as a mandatory factor in surviving current and future business environments. Those business schools that remain entrenched in their philosophies and approaches of yesterday will fail to cope with the newly emerging context of the global business world and society, in which resource constraints, climate change, and shifts in political and economic powers will affect to a great degree the ways in which people learn, earn, and survive. This assertion is not just a prediction, but a certainty reflective of the present reality changes taking place in the macro-environment of business.

Business schools that are market leaders have become that way because of their valuable human resources. In organizations, "people value" is an important factor in adding to quality and developing brand recognition. Thus, management of knowledge workers is a key factor in business schools; and where else does one find knowledge workers than in these schools that set the stage for both the theoretical and practical principles and theories underlying business activities, individual entrepreneurial spirit, and organizational transformation and growth. Business schools are made up of experts in all areas of business and leadership that shape and influence societal-wide thinking and the mind-frame of current and future entrepreneurs by advocating best practices, inventing new norms for efficiency and effectiveness, and leading change management efforts. Business schools that are followers spend more time maintaining their current platforms, while business schools that are leaders spend most time breaking away from their current constraints and "comfort zones" to create new paths to the future, thereby empowering those with whom they come into contact to think anew and develop bold visions. One of the major differences between business school leaders and followers is the degree to which they network with corporations and participate in community development and leadership. Business schools that are leaders ensure that they have a secure connection with stakeholders, such as society and the community, internal employees, customers, governmental organizations, and business partners such as their suppliers and distributors, and even some competitors. Business schools that wish to continue successfully into the upcoming tumultuous decades will need to have a combination of strategies that capitalize on their strengths in order to increase opportunities, while guarding against and eliminating threats and weaknesses that threaten their very survival and the success of their graduates.

Summary

As 21st century business schools struggle in today's highly competitive "market jungle," they must rethink their visions and strategic values. They should recognize the immediacy of change and the power they have to shape their own future while preparing for the uncertain aspects of the change process. In order to become successful leaders in the global education arena, 21st century business schools should follow several important principles:

1. Closely assess the external global environment in which they operate and restructure themselves strategically to respond to current and emerging challenges.
2. Optimize technological usage in creating and developing programs that uniquely "bridge the gap" between the theoretical and practical world while empowering knowledge workers and innovators for the working world.
3. Promote both entrepreneurial and intraprenurial spirits within individuals and organizations by developing appropriate frameworks for managing and delivering training, while maintaining sound connections with the corporate world.
4. Strive to create unique and new approaches to delivering education and training that integrate broader aspects of the practical world and theoretical world appropriate to the process of empowering graduates to "dare to be different" in their thinking and problem-solving skills and abilities.
5. Capitalize on change to create new platforms for the business world at large through innovative curriculum structure and knowledge exchanges across international cultural, social, and political domains that represent globalizing influences on business and economic survival.
6. Inculcate the values of legality, ethics and morality, and social responsibility, and instill in the students a keen sense of the legal, ethical and moral, and social responsibilities of business – for themselves, their families, and on behalf of their companies

and organizations, and their communities and society as a whole.

Chapter 2

Focus, Mission, and Distinctiveness

Business schools today, especially competitive private schools in this very difficult economic climate, clearly must provide an excellent education to their students. They must offer a wide variety of value-maximizing programs and courses to the students at times and places convenient to the students. Schools must have the freedom to operate – geographically and "virtually," that is, by modes of delivery, and should seek to be less constrained, whenever possible, by "political" factors. Schools thus should be flexible, and certainly so must be private schools that are "non-traditional," in order to reach individuals who are not in a conventional academic mode, such as working professionals. A fundamental mission of business schools is to help students find employment opportunities, particularly when jobs are scarce in a recessionary economy. Yet there is a larger goal, and that is to produce students who will be business leaders, innovators, and entrepreneurs, who will build a stronger and sustainable economy - locally and globally. This chapter[1], therefore, will discuss certain significant challenges facing business schools today, focusing on accreditation and the related area of faculty research and scholarship, as well as examine quality assurance, recruitment and retention, and diversity concerns.

---

[1] For more information on this chapter, see the original publication: Cavico, F. J. and Mujtaba, B. G. (January 2010). An assessment of business school's student retention, accreditation, and faculty scholarship challenges. *Contemporary Issues in Education Research,* 3(1), 01-13.

Introduction

The business environment for schools of business is certainly a very competitive one today. There are state schools and private schools; there are traditional, innovative, and entrepreneurial schools; there are non-profit and for-profit schools; there are ground-based and online schools; and there are combinations of the foregoing. They are all aggressively searching for students. *Business Week* in its review and rating of business schools related that almost one-half of all Executive MBA programs and part-time programs reported a decrease in enrollment for 2009 (Gloecker, 2009, pp. 48-49). There is also, despite the current economic problems, a faculty shortage, especially doctoral faculty. Moreover, due to the recessionary economy, producing less government contributions and less endowment revenues, schools are now moving into marketing areas they once eschewed. *Business Week* also pointed out that business schools, particularly those with weekend, part-time, and Executive MBA programs, "...have been transformed entirely by the economic downturn," including the significant loss of corporate sponsorships (Gloecker, 2009, p. 48). These factors amount to a "perfect storm" for business schools.

To vividly illustrate the nature of the very challenging marketplace today confronting business schools, let us relate two incidents, recently occurring on the same day. In a leading newspaper of South Florida, the *Sun-Sentinel*, of Ft. Lauderdale, there appeared a large, bright orange sticker on the cover of the paper. The sticker was in the colors of the University of Florida, located several hours away in Gainesville, advertising a new online master's program in entrepreneurship offered by that university's school of business. On the very same day, there appeared on the front page of the Marketplace section of *The Wall Street Journal* an article (Glader, 2009), titled *"The Jack Welch MBA Coming to Web,"* which discussed the former General Electric CEO's financial and advisement relationship with a very entrepreneurial school, called Chancellor University, and its incipient online MBA program. Masters of Management as well as undergraduate business degree programs are also being planned. The emphasis, as per the philosophy of Mr. Welch, will be on quality, leadership, and human resources. Such is the nature of competition facing business schools, particularly mid-tiered, tuition-driven schools, which are being "squeezed" by the more traditional schools and the newer for-profit entrepreneurial schools. When a large, traditional, state school like the University of Florida commences a specialized online business program, and then advertises the program on ground far from its "home turf," it is time for all schools to take notice. High-level strategic planning and decision-making thus must occur as to what programs and courses to offer as well as to determine which ones are draining resources so they can be dropped. A school must aggressively search out and identify market opportunities, and then seek to secure a differential competitive advantage in markets where it deems it can be successful. The keys to sustainability and growth are innovation and entrepreneurship, which mean new ideas are imperative, and some risks must be taken. A school, therefore, must be on the "leading edge of change," yet be very nimble and not fall off the edge. Flexibility is important since nobody wants the "leading edge" concept to be converted to a "bleeding edge."

Schools of business, therefore, must be able to engage students, provide them with high quality, innovative, and entrepreneurial academic experiences, and thus afford them career opportunities. Schools must consider both the traditional and non-traditional aspects of business education – and not only in delivery modes but in content too. Yet schools must be practical and first focus on programs within their capabilities that are in the greatest demand, and thus will produce immediate revenue and long-term value. To illustrate, "differentiated" MBAs, specialized MBAs, and degrees with competitive pricing, and encompassing day, evening, weekend, online, and hybrid modalities, are essential in this very competitive business and academic environment. Programs and courses could also be "blended," that is, by combining disciplines. For example, a blended business course focusing on the consumer or customer would include, in addition to the traditional marketing subject matter, material encompassing elements of psychology, sociology, economics, ethics, accounting, and information technology. Programs could have a global theme, such as global energy, finance, and economics. Students must be provided the content and skills to enable them to compete in the global marketplace. International partnership programs, particularly cross-disciplinary and MBA programs thus emerge as viable opportunities. In a global energy MBA, for example, there could be specialized MBA energy courses. Courses could be offered in "Global Finance" or "Managing the Global

Economy." These international programs and courses would demonstrate the complexity and inter-relatedness of the global economy. Due to the recessionary economic climate, attention should be paid to finance courses, such as a personal finance course for all business students (or for that matter for all the college's or university's students) or a finance and trading course for more advanced students. Leadership, the environment, and healthcare are also emerging fields and thus ripe for specialized programs. Entrepreneurship programs possess a new and critical importance as the potential and luster of a corporate career may have been dimmed. Executive MBA programs may be another viable alternative for schools. Such programs could focus on a particular company or industry, or have an international component, including an extensive field trip to a foreign country to meet with government and business leaders. Despite the recessionary economy, some schools fared well, mentioned in *Business Week*, specifically "...ones that quickly adapted to these changing economic conditions" (Gloecker, 2009 p. 49). One example of efficacious adaption is for schools to use corporate "custom" programs, which are tailored to specific companies, held at corporate sites, and are more cost effective and less expensive for a corporate sponsor than open-enrollment programs on campus.

Programs and courses could be created that would provide immediate, tangible, and measurable benefits for companies sponsoring their employees as students. In the human resources fields, courses and programs could be built around the "soft skills," such as managing "virtually" or from a distance, communication, teambuilding, mediation and arbitration, brokering compromises, avoiding conflict, dispelling rumors, and advising and mentoring. In addition to leadership and human resources, programs and courses could be developed highlighting "intrapreneurship," process management and improvement, supply chain management, and logistics, and, furthermore, these programs and courses could be geared to specific companies and industries. Another example is the "Green MBA" or "Eco-MBA," wherein students study, in addition to traditional business skills and knowledge, social and environmental issues and sustainable business practices, and thus focus on the "triple bottom-line" of "people, planet, and profit" (Brant and Ohtake, 2008). In addition to helping save the planet, another goal of "going green" is to give the students a competitive edge. The "green" programs recognize that in order to be globally competitive in today's economy, the students must have an understanding of the risks as well as opportunities that the natural environment presents to business (Locke, 2007).

Creating Business Consulting, Small Business, Entrepreneurship, Trading, and Business Ethics centers is another good way to produce value for the school and its stakeholders. The Trading Center could establish an investment fund dedicated to socially responsible investing, so as to provide to the students a unique and very practical as well as socially responsible learning experience (Alsop, 2007). The Entrepreneurship Center, in addition to advising and counseling, could have a Business Plan competition. The administration, faculty, students, business leaders, and community would be involved; valuable consulting services and guest lecturers would be provided; certificate programs, for example in entrepreneurship, innovation, and leadership, would be offered; and the reputation of the school thereby enlarged and enhanced within the community, including potential students and charitable donors. Schools, therefore, must reach out to students, and on a global basis, and with a variety of programs, joint programs, strategic alliances and partnerships; schools thus must be "comprehensive," but also cognizant of demand as well as financial ramifications and delivery capabilities. Trapnell (2009) notes that "management education is an export business for some countries" and that "partnerships and alliances are growing at a rapid pace" (p. 8).

It is critically important for schools of business to align what they plan to teach with what the students need to know to be successful. Ultimately, the students have to be shown that their education will produce value in the form of employment or entrepreneurship. Therefore, it is essential that schools build a "platform" or a foundation for learning, as well as create a stimulus for continuous learning. Schools of business must develop not only the critical analytical skills of their students, but also must foster creative and innovative thinking, so the students can be successful business leaders, managers, and entrepreneurs. A school must motivate the students and teach them how to think differently about business. What are the new markets, the new products, the new services? What are the entrepreneurial and intraprenurial opportunities? Those would be key questions to attempt to answer. The goal is for the students to be leaders and "shapers" and not mere followers and "reactors." Students must leave school thinking, and in particular asking, "How can we do things differently?"

Schools, particularly state schools and the more traditional, "bricks and mortar" private schools should be concerned about becoming too "centralized" and too conservative, and consequently creating further structural and mental impediments to change. They may now have to be a bit more innovative, entrepreneurial, and "progressive." At times, it may be easier for a school to be more traditional as opposed to innovative. Yet a school in today's environment must be very careful about being too traditional. Modern schools must abjure the old "if you build it, they will come" philosophy, because such a school will not survive in this competitive environment. A school, fundamentally, must have a "brand" – a unique and valuable and value-creating brand – one that produces excellent value for the students. The school must seek out opportunities, marshal resources, and make this brand visible and operational in clearly chosen markets, and show how this "brand" can provide a direct, immediate, and measurable return to the students (as well as their parents and perhaps corporate sponsors) for their educational investment.

Accreditation Essentials

Regional accreditation is important for a business school to be regarded as a reputable academic institution. Yet should schools of business also seek to obtain accreditation by the Association to Advance Collegiate Schools of Business (AACSB)? Is AACSB accreditation essential for successful schools of business? Is the growth for non-AACSB schools going to come from securing accreditation, or are there other options? Do the benefits of AACSB accreditation outweigh the costs? Would a school be better off in spending its money creating superior programs than seeking AACSB accreditation? Some schools may have a very good, innovative, and entrepreneurial model, and be very successful and produce successful students, without any accreditation, let alone AACSB accreditation. After all, the "marketplace is the best accreditor." The true test of a school is the marketplace; that is, if a school delivers what it promises, produces value for its students, the community, and society, and the market recognizes and rewards such value production, then the school may be as well off without accreditation, and it actually may be worse off with it. Yet the authors are not blind to the "political reality" of AACSB accreditation. So, evidently, such accreditation must be closely examined.

The first and foremost issue is the value of AACSB accreditation to a school. The authors have had many discussions with faculty colleagues and with academic administrators at their own school and other schools, especially former deans, regarding AACSB accreditation. The clear consensus is that such accreditation is regarded as synonymous with "quality" and legitimacy. The authors have repeatedly heard such descriptive phrases as "brand enhancer," "gold seal," "gold standard," "top one," "hallmark," "must have," "essential," "ticket to success," and "top level" being applied to the AACSB accreditation. Many members of the academic business community regard such certification as "imperative" for a school to be regarded as a "major player" and thus to be competitive in today's challenging academic "market."

There are, of course, other entities that rank business schools; and accordingly perhaps one can be a bit creative in "playing the rankings game," for example, by seeking out other recognitions, such as by the Wall Street Journal, Business Week, US News & World Report, and recruiters' rankings, that might be easier for a school to achieve. There are also other alternative accrediting bodies, such as the International Assembly for Collegiate Business Education (IACBE), the regional bodies such as the Southern Association of Colleges and Schools (SACS), and the newer international one, EQUIS, the European Quality Initiative for Schools. Yet there is no denying that AACSB has done an excellent job in "branding" its accreditation designation. For example, the authors have heard "talk" that there is an AACSB initiative to persuade employers not to provide tuition assistance for employees who do not attend AACSB accredited schools and, even more controversial, not to hire graduates of non-AACSB schools. Furthermore, many schools advertising for faculty, especially for doctoral and other graduate faculty, already specifically and explicitly require that the faculty candidates be graduates of AACSB accredited schools of business. Trapnell (2009), however, notes the official AACSB policy that "AACSB does not require schools hire faculty with degrees from AACSB accredited schools only" (p. 23).

Yet to even consider AACSB certification, there are many challenges for a school to overcome before it can seek AACSB accreditation, and with a realistic chance to attain such certification. The qualification of the faculty is a very important area for accreditation purposes, and AACSB is "very stringent" regarding faculty qualifications. One such difficulty for schools, particularly schools that use a great deal of part-time, adjunct professors is the AACSB standard that certain numbers of the faculty, both full- and part-time, must be "academically qualified" (AQ), and others must be "professionally qualified" (PQ). Since many adjunct professors are active practitioners in their teaching fields and possess the proper academic degree credentials, the problem for many schools will be the AQ status of the adjuncts (and perhaps some full-time faculty too) since AQ, in essence, means that the faculty must be published in peer-reviewed scholarly journals and present papers at peer-reviewed scholarly conferences. These scholarly activities are typically the work of the full-time faculty and not a school's adjunct faculty. Moreover, if a school uses adjunct professors who teach full-time at other schools, and these professors are AQ, then these faculty members might be regarded as AQ only for their "home" schools; that is, their AQ status will not transfer over to the school retaining them as adjunct professors. While it is beyond the purposes of this book to delve into the exact AQ versus PQ percentages, as well as the number of articles and presentations needed to be AQ, the authors nevertheless want to emphasize that the AQ requirement could emerge as a very difficult issue for some schools. The AQ standards very likely will be construed as much higher for doctoral teaching faculty and also higher for master's teaching faculty than undergraduate teaching faculty.

Another challenging AACSB accreditation issue related to schools using large numbers of adjunct faculty is the status and percentages of the school's faculty regarded as "actively participating." Actually, it is the authors' understanding that AACSB no longer uses the word "adjunct" but rather has a requirement that a certain percentage of the school's faculty, both full- and part-time, be actively participating in the academic life of the school, for example by sitting on faculty meetings and other committees, assisting in program and course design and revision, helping in the preparation of syllabi and selection of textbooks. Again, it is not the intent of the authors to address specific requirements, especially numerical percentages; yet it must be emphasized that a school may have to make a substantial effort to achieve that "actively participating" status for many of the part-time faculty as well as to achieve the proper number of actively participating part-time faculty. Plainly, in order to get the part-time faculty to be more active, the school may have to pay them more; or the obverse, that is, the school may reduce their numbers by hiring more full-time (and presumably actively participating as well as AQ) faculty members; yet the cost of the latter approach clearly has even greater financial ramifications for a school and its college or university. Another way to meet the AQ and "actively participating" requirements is for a school to create a Master Professor and Professional Specialist or Faculty teaching system, wherein the Master Professor, who would be a full-time, actively participating, and AQ faculty member, is the "professor of record" for a course, whose various sections would be taught by "professionally qualified" but not necessarily AQ and "actively participating" Professional Specialists (formerly called "adjuncts"). The Master Professor would supervise the Professional Specialists, produce some core lectures (either in a large lecture hall or online by video), make sure that the course syllabus, learning objectives, and exams are consistent, be available for communication with all the students, for example by chat sessions, and, most importantly, assign the students' grades. The Professional Specialists would teach the sections of the class under the supervision of the Master Professor. For this arrangement to pass AACSB muster, the Master Professor must do more than "merely" supervise, rather, he or she must actually assign the students their grades. However, since the grading is critical here, one of the author's colleagues perceptively discerned that one must be careful, especially if there are several sections to a course and a group exam, that the Master Professor "of record" does not turn into the Master Grader!

Colleagues warn that there is not a great deal of flexibility with any of these AACSB accrediting standards. Moreover, to truly complicate matters, many of the AACSB standards, in the opinion of the authors, are a bit vague and not at all precise and exact, and thus subject to interpretation (and perhaps by members of an AACSB accreditation committee who may come from very traditional schools). Nevertheless, all these standards and percentages – AQ, PQ, quality (and especially quality as that is a recurring theme of the accrediting standards), and "actively participating" – are applied not "merely" at school of business' main campus site, but rather to all branch campuses, clusters, and academic sites, and to all business programs – ground-based, online, or hybrid - delivered at these branch campuses, and sites. Are the concomitant financial ramifications fully thought out? Is a school prepared to drop its doctoral program, or its MBA program, or some of its branch campus sites in order to get the "numbers" right for programmatic accreditation. Is a school prepared to make the financial commitment to hire doctoral faculty who are AQ? Owen (2009) points out that "AACSB's push to accredit more business schools no doubt has had an effect on the number of doctorally qualified faculty that are needed" (p. 6). He also notes that the:

Dramatic increase in the number of accredited schools means that there will be more demand for doctorally qualified faculty. Since it is smaller, non-research schools that have been added since the 1992 change in AACSB standards, it also means that many (perhaps most) of these schools need to lower teaching loads, requiring even more faculty than had been necessary prior to thoughts of accreditation. Additionally, the requirement for greater numbers of doctorally qualified faculty means that there will be greater demand for faculty who are able to remain academically qualified (Owen, 2009, p. 6).

The quality of a school of business' programs is a paramount issue for AACSB. Accordingly, it again must be noted that the word "quality" continuously appears throughout the organization's accrediting criteria. This aforementioned quality standard, it has been related to the authors, is much more strictly applied to those schools seeking accreditation with doctoral programs. One former dean related that a business school that has a doctoral program "raises the AACSB bar" for accreditation. As such, the AQ percentages for doctoral faculty may be, either explicitly or implicitly, very high indeed; and the number of peer reviewed journal articles and presentations will most likely be larger for doctoral faculty. In addition, the "quality" of the scholarship for doctoral faculty will be an issue. How such quality is measured is another perplexing issue, but it should be noted that some schools rank publications as "A, B, or C" journals (there are no "D" journals). Some schools send out articles to faculty at other schools for a quality review, and yet other schools use a "citation index," whereby the direct impact of an "article" can be gauged by the number of scholarly articles that cite it, the number of schools that use it, the number of companies / managers that apply it, or even the number of times the article has been downloaded. For doctoral faculty, AACSB would expect not only higher research productivity but also higher level journals, and these are "must have" elements of certification.

There may be some "hope" for schools, particularly non-traditional schools, in seeking accreditation. Since most quality control programs tend to be "moving targets" in search of continuous improvement, similarly, AACSB has "evolved," and as a result is no longer a "one size fits all" or a "formula approach" organization, but rather is becoming more of a "big tent." As a result, AACSB may now be available for schools that are "not like other schools." This new flexibility has emerged in two key areas: the school's Mission Statement and Assurance of Learning process. An artfully crafted as well as accurate Mission Statement can provide some help to schools seeking accreditation, as a focal point of AACSB's examination of a school will be its mission statement. So, for example, take a school that is primarily a teaching school, and perhaps also not a traditional one, but rather an innovative one that uses online and hybrid formats, weekend and night programs, and branch campuses and sites in order to reach students not usually served by more traditional schools. The mission statement reflect the preceding features, and could also emphasize the practical and applied elements to the student's education, and thus the worth of practitioners as teachers and researchers might be more readily recognized. The mission statement of such a school should naturally emphasize these elements, and though the mission statement will not totally obviate AACSB standards, it should afford a school some latitude, as well as effect to the school's benefit a more liberal interpretation of AQ and research quality criteria. A mission-driven AACSB strategy, therefore, is an essential element to a school's accreditation effort.

Trapnell (2009) relates that one of the "assurances" of AACSB accreditation is that an accredited school "produces graduates who have achieved specified learning goals" (p. 10). Assurance of Learning

(AOL) emerges as a major component of accreditation, as well as one that might afford a school a bit of flexibility in seeking or maintaining accreditation. Though it is not the purpose of the authors to deal with the very important and complex topic of learning outcomes and Assurance of Learning, nonetheless some basic points must be made. First, in essence, this Assurance of Learning process seeks to ensure that school academic program goals and course learning objectives are being achieved. The process is based on creating testing items, and then assessing what the students are learning, or perhaps not learning, by pre- and post-testing. Note that this assessment should occur not merely at the course level but also at the degree and program levels. Though such assessment will involve a considerable amount of work for a school, it is naturally important to assure the school's own stakeholders as well as accrediting bodies that the students are actually learning what they are supposed to learn. One important aspect of this outcomes' examination will be to ascertain if the students are learning the objectives of the courses and the goals of the program. Trapnell (2009) underscores that for AACSB, assessment is the "key to continuous improvement," that a school must have certain learning goals, and must engage in "direct" and "systemic" assessment of learning, which can accomplished by course-embedded measures, stand-alone testing, or other selection methods (p. 31). To illustrate one way for schools to use this Assurance of Learning process to help with its accreditation efforts, consider, for example, a school with no GMAT or GRE requirements, or a school with low GMAT or GRE scores, or a school with lower GPA standards than other accredited schools. If it can be shown that the students admitted with lower scores and averages nevertheless are shown to be demonstrably learning and, even better, ultimately successful in business or the professions, then such a school could well argue that its lack of a GMAT or GRE and/or lower "numbers" should not be an impediment to accreditation. Yet, when it comes to accreditation, a school must be able to show the accrediting body its assessment and outcomes data. Merely "saying you did it" will be insufficient; rather, a school must prove its effectiveness by means of its data.

There are also risks to accreditation. A major risk to accreditation is that it might "homogenize" a school of business and thus make it bland, and eventually non-competitive. If a school has been very successful by being innovative and entrepreneurial, and is so regarded in the business and academic communities, it must be careful not to lose these important values in an effort to secure accreditation. The objective very well might be to achieve the AACSB imprimatur, yet not at the cost of a school losing its vibrancy or the values of innovation, creativity, and entrepreneurship. Otherwise, "winning" the accreditation "battle" might be only a "Pyrrhic victory."

Another serious risk is that some of the faculty might view seeking AACSB accreditation as a threat as opposed to an opportunity. Faculty, as human beings, likely will have a certain "comfort level" with the status quo. This status quo may include a very loose or lax or non-existent scholarship policy. Change, therefore, particularly such an accreditation effort, may engender worry, dismay, or even anger. This fear and disquietude must be addressed by the school administration and the faculty as a whole. The "opportunity" element must be emphasized, and accordingly it must be stated plainly that everyone can make a contribution, everyone has a role to play, and everyone therefore will be proud when accreditation is attained. As emphasized, faculty support is critical for accreditation success. Actually, the ideal situation would be for the impetus for accreditation to have come "up" from the faculty, and not "down" from the school's administration. In addition to impeding a school's "culture" for entrepreneurship and innovation, a school must also be very careful that an accreditation effort does not disturb, hinder, or destroy a culture of collegiality among the faculty members. Accreditation, therefore, must be faculty "driven" and the faculty thus must be included in any initial accreditation feasibility studies. Everyone must be "on board" with the mission of the school and university.

Another risk of AACSB accreditation is that it may hinder innovation and entrepreneurship in the area of joint programs, for example, with a school's medical, nursing, science, and engineering schools. Combining the aforementioned fields with business in a joint degree program could be a "win-win" scenario for the students, the schools, the university, and the community. However, one must be cognizant of AACSB requirements that these joint programs, in order to be called "business" programs, must have certain percentages of business school faculty teaching the courses and these faculty must meet AACSB's AQ and "actively participating" requirements.

In looking at the number and names of schools of business accredited by the AACSB, one can see in addition to the large, established state schools and other well-recognized private schools, possessing excellent reputations, many other schools, not as well known, established, or prestigious, which nonetheless have achieved the very prestigious AACSB label. Such a fact militates against a charge that the accrediting body is "elitist"; yet it should be pointed out, as the discerning reader has already perceived, that it will be much easier for a smaller school, primarily undergraduate, with not many academic campuses or sites from the main campus, to attain AACSB status since the "correct" numbers of actively participating, AQ faculty will be easier to obtain. The bigger and more far-flung a school is, and the more graduate programs it has, and especially if it has a doctoral program, the greater the hurdles will emerge that will have to be overcome in order for a school to "win the race" for AACSB certification. The AACSB might be less stringent in applying its standards to a school with an undergraduate program only, or perhaps a small master's one, rather than schools with large graduate programs, particularly doctoral programs. There also may be an inherent conflict between a school's desire to have a more practitioner-oriented faculty and AACSB faculty standards. So, Maidment, Coleman, and Bazan (2009) in their study of Executive MBA programs (EMBA) note that since "…EMBA programs tend to be pragmatic and applied in nature, it would be interesting to see if more practitioners could be deployed to the EMBA classroom. Doing so might provide an even more applied focus in certain courses and might help conserve the load credit of full-time faculty for other activities" (p. 7). Nonetheless, they warn that "if this alternative is considered, the standards for professional qualifications of the AACSB would have to be fully considered" (Maidment, Colemand, and Bazan, 2009, p. 7).

There are, therefore, many challenging questions that will arise in a school's quest for AACSB status. Consequently, difficult decisions will have to be made by the school and university as to whether AACSB accreditation, or any alternative accreditation, makes sense for the school of business and the university. The authors, as emphasized, are not AACSB experts by any means; but they certainly would advise that before a school considers such an accreditation that the faculty and school administration, and the college or university administration, as well as other school "stakeholders," are completely aware of the work involved and the financial implications of seeking accreditation for the school and college or university, and that all the school's "stakeholders" are fully committed to the process. The costs have to be counted; and sacrifices may have to be made. AACSB accreditation is an "end" but it is also a "means" to an end, and thus must be an integral part of a school and university's strategic plan. It should be noted that seeking AACSB accreditation could involve a "tremendous cost" in resources, and might even "destroy" a school's successful business model. Consequently, the authors would strongly advise that before a school and university even entertain the prospect of the business school seeking AACSB status, the school should hire an AACSB consultant or an advisory board to advise them, and then later on, if the process is initiated, an AACSB "mentor" to further counsel the school. Yet no consultant or mentor can advise as to AACAB accreditation unless the school and university ascertain what the financial "hit" will be. What is the old military saying, still very true in this academic "battle": "What general goes to war without counting the cost"?

Faculty Research and Scholarship

Faculty research and scholarship are naturally very important activities at a school of business, and, as noted, they emerge as essential activities for a school seeking programmatic accreditation (such as IACBE or AACSB). Scholarship is so important since everything in business, in essence, is transitional, so the faculty must stay current. For example, as is well known to the readers of this book, a textbook, due to the lengthy process of publication, is really "old" when published. Scholarship supplies intellectual stimulation, thereby forcing faculty to keep thinking and to keep asking questions – questions that will be asked of the students. Scholarship is important not merely in and of itself in producing knowledge but also in making one a better teacher. Scholarship, therefore, is a critical part of good teaching, especially in today's world of fast-moving and rapid changes.

Yet what is the proper degree of research and writing? The answer depends on the nature of the business school. There is clearly a difference between a primary research type business school, where scholarship is extremely important, and a middle-ground or mid-tier school, where there is a balance between teaching and research, and a primarily teaching type of business school. In even the latter type of teaching school, the authors nevertheless strongly believe that some research and scholarship by the faculty is important and thus necessary in order to keep the faculty current and to enhance the quality of their teaching. At the undergraduate and master's levels, scholarship can be more of the "applied" type of research and writing, particularly with a company or industry focus; whereas at the doctoral level the focus of the scholarship should be creating new knowledge. The authors believe that some academic scholarship, though valuable in the "halls of academe," may be a bit too "pure," that is, arcane and abstruse, for practical business use, and consequently such research does not have a direct positive impact on society. Certain business school professors, it seems, know more about academic publishing than they do about the real-world problems in the workplace. The goal, the authors believe, is to produce scholarship that is regarded as an intellectual contribution, but also contains an "applications" component so that the scholarship is regarded as valuable and value-producing by the marketplace. Showing managers and teaching students how to manage, that is, how actually to accomplish objectives with and through employees and other people, should be a duly recognized part of academic scholarship as well as teaching. Such "real-life" research keeps a faculty member "engaged," and as a result makes him or her better in the class as well was more valuable to the business and management community. Even consulting by faculty members certainly should be permitted if it is valuable to the client and produces value to the marketplace. The authors firmly believe that business school faculty should always have a connection to the business community; such a nexus will make the faculty members' research as well as teaching more relevant and valuable. However, regarding consulting, one principal goal of consulting would be to convert the consulting endeavor, which could be writing an economic impact statement or working with a start-up on an IPO, into a peer-reviewed journal article or case study. A faculty member, therefore, could develop a portfolio of intellectual contributions that combined peer-reviewed journal articles, presentations at conferences (which ideally should be peer-reviewed and then published in full or at the least abstract form in the proceedings of the conference), books, book chapters, and book reviews, and case studies (preferably peer-reviewed, of course). Yet research and writing, as with all activities in a school of business, must be in alignment with the mission, vision, and principles of the school as well as the school's accreditation requirements, and it must also conform to a mission-driven definition of "quality." Trapnell (Personal Communication at the Academy of Business Disciplines Conference, November 07, 2009) explains that regarding research, it is AACSB's goal to "encourage research that matches a school's mission and has the intended *impact*...for practitioner/industry applications for student learning for knowledge/theory development" (Trapnell, p. 28). Trapnell also notes that a "pilot project" is underway to determine how the "impact" of research and scholarship will be measured (2009, p. 28). A key question to answer, related to the school's mission, is what "market" the faculty member is writing to. Is the research highly theoretical that is valued by "pure" academics, or is it practical and applied, relevant to business and thus of value to a corporation and the industry? Moreover, as a very practical matter, it must be pointed out that a school of business may not have the resources necessary to support a faculty member who wishes to publish theoretical type of research in a "top" journal. As emphasized, a school must be very clear and certain as to its mission, the viability of its mission in the marketplace, and the school and university resources necessary to fulfill that mission.

Any scholarship is, of course, related to the teaching course "load" of the faculty. Generally speaking, it seems that the standard norm is three courses for nine credits for each of the two traditional semesters for a total of 18 credits a year (with opportunities for additional summer teaching perhaps). However, that typical teaching responsibility could (and should in the authors' opinion) be further reduced for faculty teaching at the master's and especially the doctoral level, where the scholarship requirements in both quantity and quality will be more demanding. Course reductions for scholarship could always be considered on an individual basis, though granting such teaching releases may be constrained by economic considerations. Moreover, at some schools, support for scholarship is very tangible; as such, there are cash incentives, for example, point systems are used to compensate a faculty member who produces a certain amount of scholarship, and when a certain number of points are achieved the faculty member is given a course release or a monetary payment equivalent to teaching one "overload" course. Other schools simply make payments for peer reviewed journal articles deemed to be disciplined-based and/or "valuable" to academics or practitioners. Nevertheless, it also must be pointed out that AACSB officials tend to "frown" upon a doctoral faculty member teaching a faculty "load" which is in most schools the usual undergraduate teaching "load." There thus should be a relationship between teaching "load" and research productivity, and particularly for a faculty member designated as "research faculty."

The authors have always felt that faculty should be encouraged to be active researchers and to publish by support and positive reinforcements, such as reduced teaching "loads," training, especially as to research methods and statistics, mentoring, collaboration, support for attending conferences, research and editing support, and further support to convert paper presentations at conferences into peer-reviewed journal articles. One way to produce scholarship is to engage a faculty member in an area of real interest to the faculty member; that is, find out what the faculty member cares about and what he or she has a passion for; next, match the faculty member to this business area or entity; and then encourage the faculty member to do some research; and finally help the faculty member publish the results of this research as an article or case study. Collaborative efforts naturally should be encouraged in this endeavor. The "carrot," therefore, the authors firmly believe, is better than the "stick"; yet the authors are cognizant of the fact that some schools may utilize the "stick," in the form of denial of promotions or summer teaching work, in order to "encourage" research and writing. It may be necessary to produce scholarship, especially as part of an accreditation effort, to "ruffle some feathers" with the faculty. At the very least, if any "ruffling" is to be done, or any "stick" is to be used, it is imperative that the school administration inform the faculty of the policy, explain it, and state the rationales behind the policy, and not merely "imperially" announce it to the faculty.

Economics and Quality Assurance

A principal purpose of a business school is to create value – for the students, the school, and all the school's stakeholders; and value is "simply" quality divided by cost! There are, obviously, many ways to measure quality, but one very good and practical approach is to demonstrate how successful the school's students have been. Yet a school needs students to begin with! A school should not just lower standards to increase the number of students, as that approach is a very short-sighted one. The key, the authors feel, is to create programs and courses that possess quality and respond to the needs of the marketplace. In order to respond to the needs of the market, a school must be agile, flexible, and responsive to the marketplace, which now is a very crowded and competitive arena. The assertion that there is a direct and inverse relationship between quality and quantity is a false premise in the authors' opinion. When dealing with quality and economic considerations, one must take a long-term approach, define the school's mission, vision, and core principles correctly, create the correct strategy, and then implement the right tactics to achieve the strategy, in particular the right type of marketing to the proper segments of the community. By doing so, the authors believe that quality and quantity are not trade-offs, but rather, with some judicious balancing, both can be attained in the long-run. Yet it must be noted that this balancing is an "art" as well as a "science"!

Another method to create value and to sustain economic viability, while ensuring quality, is to use technology in creative ways. The students today surely are very comfortable with technological systems. However, the authors feel that academic programs should not be just delivered online; rather there should be some face-to-face contact and socialization and networking opportunities for the students. One approach would be to use "hybrid" or "blended" programs that have ground contact but also a strong technology program. Actually such hybrid programs might be used creatively to encompass courses taught by academic faculty (who are AQ and actively participating) as the teachers "of record" supplemented by professional faculty and business leaders. Another related approach to recruitment and retention is the convenience factor, that is, the school should seek to bring education to the students, especially students not usually served by more traditional schools, for example, by online systems, of course, but also by weekend, evening, and off-campus programs, including branch campuses, cluster sites, and corporate sites. However, it is critical to point out that the education delivered and the quality thereof at all these sites and by all these modalities must be the same, particularly for accreditation purposes.

Recruitment, Retention, and Diversity

Finding, recruiting, and retaining students, while maintaining quality, are not easy tasks. Owen (2009) states that the assumption that student enrollments at schools of business will continue to rise, as they did in the late 1990's, may be erroneous. The reason Owen gives is simple and straightforward – the deteriorating economy. Employability is the key factor, and the recent rising unemployment and continuing layoffs consequently will reduce business student enrollments, especially of finance majors and MBA students. Owen (2009) reports "declining" MBA applications, and he predicts "dramatically fewer finance majors in the future" (p. 7). One solution to this decreasing student enrollment is to create and offer differentiated and specialized programs that are exciting and innovative, and that allow the students to grow and develop. Making the educational opportunities available to the students at convenient times and places, either by ground sites (whether branch campuses, academic centers, cluster sites, or corporate sites) or in an online format, is an important ingredient to recruitment and retention. School administrators should also make sure that faculty and advisors have a flexible schedule to match the needs of traditional as well as online and hybrid students that need career development coaching. Career services have always been very important for a school to provide, usually for undergraduate and full-time graduate students. However, as a result of the deteriorating economy, *Business Week*, in its 2009 review and rating of business schools (Gloecker, 2009), noted that many typically employed weekend, part-time, and Executive MBA students have lost their jobs or are very fearful of losing their jobs. Consequently, these students are expecting and demanding job counseling and placement services that usually were reserved for full time students. The flexibility of a school's programs is an important "selling" point, especially for working adults, and particularly for MBA programs, which could be one year, full-time, or two years in an evening, weekend, or online format, or in a hybrid ground and online format. Another key factor will be to demonstrate to potential students (as well as their parents and also the companies that furnish their tuition) that their education will provide relevant, immediate, direct, and measurable value to themselves and their companies; and that they will thus receive an immediate return for their tuition dollars.

Companies must be shown that by funding students they will receive a more educated, knowledgeable, and skillful workforce, and thus receive a return on their educational investment in their employees. Offering specialized certificate type programs that target industries where education is in high demand, such as health care, emerges as a good tactic, not only to attract executive education type students, but also to convert some of them to traditional students as well as to establish corporate "cluster sites" at their companies. International recruiting should of course be considered, and joint programs with foreign schools may be a way to bring in those and more students to one's school. Yet, as noted, a school must be sure that the standards for admission and graduation for foreign students must be the same as the school's "regular" students; otherwise, accreditation problems could ensue. Many schools establish relationships and alliances with community colleges whose students can transfer over to a school in their junior year. Deans and associate deans should visit community colleges on a regular basis to "show the flag." Programs also could be established as "cohort" programs where the students, particularly graduate students would take all of the same courses on the same sequence, thereby creating a common personal, academic, professional and networking bond. Schools should "spotlight" faculty and students who can reach out to the community, and thus schools should produce community events that highlight students, especially minority students. The media, especially the very cost effective community radio networks, should be used to advertise the school and its programs. Such advertising, however, should "stay on point," and thus emphasize programs where the school has a clear, differentiated, competitive advantage. Yet, at a more basic level, schools should use students to bring in their friends as potential students for the school. A school web page could be created with vignettes by students. Schools could also attract students, as well as burnish their reputation in the community, by using speakers, on ground but also on the radio where a business show could be created, with certain (and compensated) faculty speaking on a current topic and answering questions, or with business entrepreneurs being identified and interviewed. The goals, of course, are to enhance the school's reputation, obtain good students (and then to keep them), as well as to do some "friend-raising" which hopefully will lead to some successful fund-raising.

The authors cannot sufficiently emphasize how important "customer service," advising and counseling, and mentoring are when it comes to the students staying in school and having a good and productive educational experience. It is imperative that students can talk to a real person, whether a faculty member, advisor, or the dean him or herself. The "human element" is critical. Prospective students could be briefly introduced to faculty members, and perhaps a faculty member or even the dean himself or herself could conduct the tour of the business school. Providing academic assistance to the students, for example, in the form of tutorials, writing and language labs, and technology workshops, is also very important. Outreach to the community is essential, particularly for attracting minority, women, and other under-represented students. Achieving a diverse student body may be difficult for some schools, perhaps just due to geography; but such a goal is a very laudable one for the school and a very beneficial result for all the students. Perhaps a rural or suburban school could do some recruiting in the central cities in order to seek out under-represented students. Diversity should be part of the normal academic process for a school and university. The idea is to create a true learning global community that is diverse, multi-national, multi-cultural, and multi-lingual; and thus a community that reflects the "real world" the students will live and do business in. There even could be a business college dorm but with a diverse business major student body. The fact that the students have similar interests would be most helpful in acclimating the students, especially the international students, to campus life, and as such would provide a support and networking system. The benefits of having a diverse student body for all the students are well known. Yet one problem for schools that have been successful in attracting minority students is that in these difficult economic times some of these students may not have the financial ability to commence, and then continue with, their studies. One solution is the use of scholarships and grants, of course; and a solution for those that have dropped out is for schools to create "reclamation" programs with reduced tuition and substitute courses.

Advising and counseling students are critical activities for a school, obviously, and all faculty members must take part in such efforts. Small classes are of course desirable, but such small size can be problematic in difficult economic times. Yet even if undergraduate classes are very large, nonetheless there can be supplemental lectures online as well as "breakout" sessions with professional specialists and business leaders so as to combine theory and practice.

Summary

The business environment for schools of business is certainly a very competitive one today. Business schools of the 21st century must provide an excellent education to their students through creativity, quality assurance, and uniqueness. A fundamental mission of business schools is to help students find employment opportunities, particularly when jobs are scarce in a recessionary economy. Yet there is a larger goal, and that is to produce students who will be business leaders, innovators, and entrepreneurs, who will build a stronger and sustainable economy locally and globally. Today's business schools, therefore, must offer a wide variety of engaging, distinctive, and value-maximizing programs and courses to the students at times, places, and modalities convenient to the students. Schools thus should be flexible, and certainly so must be private schools that are "non-traditional," in order to reach individuals who have been under-represented academically or who are not in a conventional academic mode, such as working professionals.

Chapter 3

Leadership and Morality

The dean is the leader of the school of business. This chapter will examine the essential attributes of leadership in the context of business schools. Critical components of effective leadership are ethics, morality, and integrity. This chapter[2], accordingly, will examine the dean's responsibility as the leader of the school to reflect and impart these core values. The chapter also will discuss the business school's role in inculcating these values to the students. Accordingly, the authors, based on their own experiences, provide an example of a graduate level business ethics course. Finally, this chapter will emphasize and justify why it is a moral imperative today for schools of business to inculcate these ethical values to the students.

Introduction

Admittedly, being a dean is not an easy job by any means. The position a dean may find himself or herself is that a dean "can't afford to make a mistake at a tuition-driven institution." One important role of a dean as well as associate and assistant deans at schools of business is to support the faculty and staff, to help to develop them, and to make them successful. Listening and communication are of course critical, and consensus should always be sought, yet a dean must be prepared when necessary to do some serious "prioritizing," and then to make the "tough" decisions. Communication also allows the faculty and administration to learn of problems ahead-of-time; and a joint

---

[2] For more information on this chapter, see the original publication: Cavico, F. J. and Mujtaba, B. G. (2009). The State of Business Schools, Business Education, and Business Ethics. *Journal of Academic and Business Ethics*, 2, pp. 1-7.

recognition and understanding of problems should produce more efficacious solutions. Arthur G. Bedeian warns of deans succumbing to the "dean's disease" (Bedeian, 2002). This deleterious situation arises when: "…deans become isolated from dissenting voices as sycophants vie for personal gains. The ready acquiescence and flattery that accompany such competitions can easily lead deans to believe that their ideas are superior to those of their faculty….As a consequence, deans are effectively insulated from day-to-day realities, neither aware that they do not understand what is going on in their colleges nor that their lack of truthful information may be having negative effects" (Bedeian, 2002, p. 165).

Governance at many schools of business is regulated, of course, by union collective bargaining agreements. At other schools, there are tenure or long-term contracts, as well as a faculty senate, and faculty committee arrangements, with contractual rights and responsibilities. At non-union and non-tenure schools, there always will emerge the important issue of "governance." There always must be at least a healthy and free debate among the faculty and between the faculty and the dean and administration, where academic colleagues can disagree (though not be disagreeable). The objective should be for the faculty to agree to a policy, or at the very least understand the rationales for it. A policy should not be merely "decreed" from "above" by the dean or the school administration to the faculty. Therefore, it is very important to build trust between the faculty and the administration, and the dean of the business school must take the lead in building trust. Building trust involves ethics, honesty, and integrity, of course, and a new dean will build up such trust gradually; yet once such trust is achieved, then decisions can be more easily made and more readily accepted.

A dean, especially a new dean, has to be aware of a school's "culture," and as such must be prepared to be patient, to listen, to consult, to be advised, and to understand; a dean should think in terms of managing the school as a process to be shared with others; yet a dean ultimately must be willing to make, and to make alone, the difficult decisions that are necessary to move the school of business forward. Bedeian (2002) advises: "…a culture should be created where people take pride in the accomplishments of one another and in which competence in others is not threatening. For such a culture to emerge requires that a dean practice a leadership that favors free discourse rather than tightly controlled discussion, nonjudgmental attitudes rather than highly defensive posturing and divergent rather than convergent thinking. An open leadership style of this nature is crucial for fostering a healthy climate where the dean's disease cannot flourish. What distinguishes first class deans from dysfunctional deans is the ability to not just to tolerate, but also to encourage dissenting ideas from a diverse group of faculty" (p. 169).

Leadership Essentials

A business school dean must be both an "open" leader as well as a good manager to be successful; yet being a leader is paramount to being a business leader such as the dean of a school of business. Yet in order to avoid the leader's "pitfalls of power" and to ward off "dean's disease," Bedeian (2002) counsels that a dean should reflect on the following questions:

1. Are you accessible to the faculty? What forums for communication exist at your school? Do you invite candid feedback from faculty and staff? Do you foster a culture that encourages faculty and staff to speak up in a frank and honest manner?

2. Do you listen? Have you promoted a culture that values expertise and intelligence over rank and title?

3. Do you frequently find it necessary to use power associated with your position instead of power derived from personal respect and academic credibility? How difficult would it be for you to resume your academic career?

4. Is there a clear and strong set of values at your school?

5. Is there a unity of purpose at your school, or is it a situation of "us" against "them" or the faculty against you?

6. Do faculty members at your school spend as much time away from the office as possible? Do hiring, promotion, and tenure decisions reflect your personal preferences or those of the faculty?

7. Is there a university-sanctioned process for fully and honestly reviewing your performance as dean? Does this review include faculty, staff, and all of the school's stakeholders?

8. How realistic is your view of the school's future? Is this view shared by the school's faculty? Are you losing touch with faculty concerns and interests?
9. Do you continue to read professional journals in your own area of expertise and interest? How recently have you taught an undergraduate course (Bedeian, 2002, p. 171)?

Bedeian (2002) advises that consideration of these aforementioned issues should help a dean realize the risks of isolation and separateness, particularly from the dean's former faculty colleagues.

A dean as the leader of a school of business has the principal duty to create and to articulate a great vision for the school and its constituent groups. The vision must be important, noble, engrossing, and achievable. It must highlight an idea or image of what the school should do in the future, as well as display the manner in which the school will realize its vision. The dean also must fulfill the concomitant responsibility of forming the school's mission and core values and principles, which, of course, must cohere with the university's vision. The vision, together with the school's mission and values, will supply the basis for a strong and effective educational enterprise. Vision, mission, and values clearly must tell the school's constituent groups what the school represents and what principles govern it. The vision, mission, and values, moreover, will furnish settled standards for evaluating the school's educational operations and practices, as well as for bringing them into alignment with the expressed purposes and direction of the university. The vision, mission, and values, finally, will serve as a motivating, concentrating, coordinating, integrating, and governing force for the individual employees and students of the school. The natural result will be a highly vitalized and effective educational institution. Another key dimension to leadership by a dean is the communication and explanation of the vision, mission, and values to all the school's stakeholders. Academic leadership, in this dimension, is viewed as a "pure" education function, especially as some stakeholder groups may not initially or directly comprehend the necessity for change, or a longer-term viewpoint, or a more expansive perspective. The business school's leader, in addition, not only must communicate and explain the vision, mission, and values, but he or she also must communicate, and demonstrate, the school's commitment to its vision, mission, and values.

The dean as leader of the school not only must get the school's stakeholders to pay attention to the school's vision, mission, and values, but also must secure, especially on the part of the school's faculty and staff, their acceptance and adoption of the vision, mission, and values. Such acceptance and adoption can be obtained, and voluntarily too, when the school's vision, mission, and values are in accord with the personal plans, aspirations, and principles of the faculty and staff and other constituent groups. The school's stakeholders then can see clearly that their own personal growth and success are very closely connected to, and perhaps to a degree dependent upon, the business school's development and prosperity. When the school's faculty and staff, in essence, elect to adopt and be bound by its vision, mission, and values, which are in alignment with their own, their self-interest will activate them to attain the vision, implement the mission, and articulate and act in accordance with the school's and university's values. The vision, mission, and values of the school thus will emerge as a real source of organizational power as well as a key criterion for decision-making.

The school of business leader's role requires that the dean focus, channel, and enliven the energies, knowledge, and talents of the faculty and staff, as well as other relevant constituents, on the firm's vision, mission, and values. The vision and mission will decide and animate the school's strategy, policy, and method; and its values will ensure the propriety and consistency of its tactics and actions. It is necessary, of course, for the dean to manifest enthusiasm, positive energy, and passion, as well to exhibit confidence, conviction, and determination. One assured way to animate the faculty and staff to achieve the vision, accomplish the mission, and comport themselves by the values, all based on shared goals, beliefs, and principles, is to set lofty yet achievable goals, challenge and encourage them to reach these objectives, believe in and trust the employees to carry out their projects, and reward them for their success and accomplishments. The dean as business leader, therefore, must create an organizational environment of opportunity, endeavor, and growth. The dean's job, however, is not necessarily to command, but rather to set elevated standards, and then to expect and insist on high levels of performance from the employees. Such a demanding attitude on the part of a leader will produce superior performance, as well as personal fulfillment, on the part of the faculty and staff, which indeed will insure the long-term success of the school and university. Truly great leaders not only induce and motivate their employees to perform, they also inspire people to work together, sacrifice, persevere, dedicate themselves, overcome resistance, and in turn become leaders themselves in order to realize the vision and accomplish the mission. Inspiration is predicated on trust, commitment to fundamental, shared values, and a belief in people- their worth, potential, and dignity; it is produced by providing hope and meaning to people, principally by demonstrating that their goals and own personal vision can be realized through the business entity's objectives. Such inspired, vision-focused, mission-centered, and values-based business leadership surely will effectuate positive, beneficial, and necessary change.

There are, of course, differences between leadership and management. The chief function of the dean as a leader is to create and to communicate the school's vision, mission, and core values, and the principal purpose of a manager is to act to achieve the stated ends in accordance with the firm's values. The dean as the school of business leader plays a critical role to the school's long-term success. The dean keeps the vision and mission continually and distinctly in view, provides the values-based direction, guidance, advancement, commitment, and frame of reference, builds and makes stronger the organization's people, resources, culture, and health, and deals with the school's "top-," as well as "bottom-line"; that is, the efficacy, results, and success of the school's policies and practices in realizing its vision, achieving its mission, and living up to its values. A manager, however, is predominantly more of a "bottom-line" person. He or she develops and articulates structures, policies, and procedures, organizes, coordinates, and controls people and resources, and focuses on speed, efficiency, logistics, and cost-benefit calculation in order to make systems work, complete selected work projects, and to achieve certain, shorter-term, business objectives. Yet, the dividing line between leading and managing is not a precisely drawn one; and leading and managing are not mutually exclusive business endeavors. A dean, therefore, is not only a leader of change, but also a good manager. That is, in order to be a successful leader, a school of business dean must play a critical role in implementing the vision that the dean has created, specifically by engaging the participation of others, typically other high-level academic administrators and faculty department heads or chairs, as leaders, and by delegating to these manager-leaders sufficient power and authority for them to play a greater leadership role. They not only adopt, together with the other stakeholders, the dean's vision and firm's mission and values, but also act as leaders themselves to their own faculty and students. Thus, these empowered leader-managers fulfill not only an implementation function, but also formulation, communication, and motivational roles. Business school leadership, therefore, emerges as the highest form of management; and leadership is revealed as an inclusive, sharing, trusting, empowering, supportive, mutually rewarding, and self-strengthening endeavor.

A principal function of an academic or business leader, as underscored, is to develop and enunciate a vision. Yet the vision must reflect an ideal and worthwhile image of the future and the mission of the school and university, and must contain high moral purposes. The values and goals manifested in the vision must be legitimate and rightful ones. Only then will the vision be an encompassing, inspiring, transcending, and transforming one. The inherent morality of the vision, the success of leadership, as well as the effective exercise of authority, fundamentally depend on the personal character of the dean as a business school and business leader. The dean not only must possess intelligence, common sense, competence, and resolution, but also integrity, honesty, trustworthiness, fairness, and morality. The successful dean, moreover, must have the personal strength of character to do consistently and diligently what is morally right. The words and actions of the leader completely must be harmonious. If a business person, manager, or academic lacks knowledge or capability, he or she always can seek education and training; but if one does not possess and demonstrate personal integrity and justness, one never will be able to establish, or perhaps rebuild, relationships of trust, which are absolutely essential to successful leadership in business, business education, or otherwise. The presence, therefore, of such an ethics-centered, highly principled leader is indispensable to the success of a school of business or any organization.

Leaders respect people! An essential component to leadership is that leaders adhere to the fundamental ethical principle of respect for people. Leaders treat people with dignity, as worthwhile, valuable "ends" in and of themselves, and definitely not as mere "means" or assets or resources. Leaders know that people are human beings, not just economic beings. Respect embraces concern and consideration, not only for the leader's followers, or the business leader's employees, but also for all affected stakeholders. The dean as an ethical business leader, therefore, will propose, direct, and effectuate beneficial change that is responsive to and respectful of all the school's constituency groups, including the university, community, and society. Respect also entails treating people equitably and managing people by a set of just principles and fair processes. Respect, finally, involves listening to people, truly communicating with people, addressing their concerns, incorporating their ideas, developing their potential, and sharing power with them. Ethical business leaders recognize people as capable of great accomplishments. Such respect will forge bonds of trust and foster a sense of moral community and worthwhile endeavor, all necessary elements to successful business leadership. The dean as a business leader must direct and guide the faculty and staff and other constituent groups in accord with a demonstrable set of ethical principles and moral rules, embodied, for example, in a school's code of ethics. Such a moral law, naturally in harmony with the school's and university's vision and mission, not only will give people confidence, motivate and inspire them, but also empower them to make decisions and lead others in a principled manner. Leadership requires the full inclusion and utmost efforts of followers, especially faculty and staff. People indeed will follow and exert themselves for those they trust, and people instinctively trust individuals who possess honesty and integrity, manifest respect for others, strive for legitimate goals, and govern themselves and others in accordance with rightful principles. Leadership emanates from trust, and trust is predicated on shared moral vision, proper common objectives, and mutual correct treatment.

Faculty and staff who trust their dean, and who are guided and governed by rightful purposes and principles, will feel authorized to achieve worthwhile objectives. Such people will possess a sense of stewardship; that is, they will act effectively to accomplish communal goals, govern themselves and others accordingly, and convince others to lead and make a contribution. A successful dean is committed to this principle of opportunity and shared leadership; and he or she will empower, encourage, and educate followers and employees to act, to lead, to bring out the best in themselves and others, and to achieve personal and organizational success. Such a discerning, encompassing, and enabling conception of leadership is also a most efficacious one. Ethical leaders value themselves and value personal as well as organizational success, yet they are altogether morally astute and enlightened to subordinate themselves to noble purposes, ethical principles, rightful conduct, as well as to shared aspirations, communal values, and manifold contributions. The challenge for a leader is to align his or her personal goals with the goals of the school, university, or organization, and also with the needs and aspirations of the leader's followers and employees, and to ensure that this alignment is centered on a crux of morality and legitimacy. Only then can a leader – academic dean or otherwise - truly lead and thereby achieve permanent positive transformation.

Business, Business Schools, and Business Ethics

One very important mission of business schools today is to "look inwardly"; that is, the school – administration, faculty, and students – must ask some piercing questions, to wit: What caused all these banking, finance, and real estate scandals? What put business and the economy in this bad situation? What role did business play in this economic recession? The objective, of course, is to provide answers that will prevent future scandals, and thus build a stronger and more sustainable economy for the United States and globally.

According to James Rest, education is the strongest correlate to and predictor of cognitive moral development and ethical maturity (Haung, 2006, p. 56). Heron (2007) underscored that cognitive moral development is considered to be "one of the critical personal characteristics influencing the entire ethics decision-making process" (p. 82). Furthermore, according to Newbaum et al. (2009), "we also know that ethics can be taught, and that educational programs that integrate the study of ethical theory with its practical application can be highly effective" (p. 21). Bloodgood, Turnley, and Mudwick (2008) state: "Prior research suggests that ethics instruction has the potential to make people less likely to engage in unethical behavior. For example, various forms of training and interventions are able to increase moral reasoning for some individuals" (p. 558).

Ethics education, therefore, is certainly a growing concern today. Yet why should colleges and universities teach business ethics? Many schools today, especially business schools, have now made ethics courses a compulsory part of the curriculum. Blood, Turnley, and Mudwick (2008) state that "...prior research indicates that university classes on "business ethics" and "business and society"...may improve ethical understanding and attitudes" (p. 558). One important perspective for the AACSB is that an "emphasis on ethics and integrity in the operations of business programs and in curricula is expected" (Trapnell, 2009, p. 33). If society is concerned about the behavior of its business people, then it is quite appropriate that a business ethics course becomes a required course in business school curriculum. Companies also must emphasize ethics and moral behavior on the part of their executives, managers, and employees. Otherwise, any perceived immoral conduct may cost a firm severely in terms of its reputation or even survival. Mujtaba (1996) explained that "there are many formats in which ethics training can be delivered to the associates of an organization. Some common ethics training sessions are being delivered through seminars, lectures, role-playing exercises, multimedia training or case studies, memos, and employee codes of conduct programs. This training should be delivered by ethicists or professional facilitators who are familiar with the firms' prospective ethical issues and challenges" (p. 169). Furthermore, Mujtaba (1996) recommends that in order to promote high ethical standards and reduce or even eliminate unfair practices in any business or industry, executives and managers should receive training and education in the following areas: 1) Individuals should receive training and instructions in the systems of justice and equity based on their corporate culture, legal system, and society. They should be made aware of the prevailing laws, regulations, and practices that govern their conduct. They should also be encouraged to go above and beyond the laws to make decisions that are moral and positively affect the lives of other people. 2) They should be made well aware of their own and their associates' legal and ethical rights, obligations, expectations, and responsibilities. These expectations and responsibilities need to be communicated to all the firm's stakeholders. 3) Executives and managers should be continuously reminded of the standards of objectivity, fairness, integrity, and maturity, as well as the need to have consideration for others and the courage to stand for what they believe is right. They should be taught persistently high standards of legal and moral behavior, which embody integrity, self-respect, justice and fairness in their relationships with everyone, personally and professionally. They must be the role models in the organization; and accordingly they must behave exactly in the manner that they would want their finest associates to behave. If each individual in the company acts with honesty and integrity, then the company's reputation will take of itself. 4) Executives and managers should be guided to, and supported in making decisions that emphasize responsiveness and accountability to the truth. They should also be instructed to avoid using their position and title to perpetuate sole self-interest or mere private gain. Thus, they should legally and morally promote value, not only for themselves, but also for their firms, its stakeholders, and society in general.

Assuming that ethics education is very important and relevant today, what should be taught, and how should ethics be taught? Bateman (1998) explained that "a common problem raised regarding the teaching of ethics is actually two-fold: how to do it and where to put it" (p. 70). Bateman (1998) also points out that "the purpose of ethics education is to make students more aware of ethical dilemmas that arise in the workplace and to prepare them to reason through the consequences of alternative courses of action" (pp. 133-34). Bateman (1998) underscores that business ethics education should stimulate the students' moral awareness and imagination, help them recognize moral issues in business and otherwise, provide to the students ethical theories and principles, and help the students develop moral reasoning skills. Buell (2009) related that "surveys of business schools show a wide range of pedagogical approaches to teaching business ethics" (p. 67). Buell explained:

Many institutions rely upon structured lectures. This approach relies on imparting information followed by discussion. Other approaches by institutions include understanding ethical concepts and reasoning by themselves...Following this approach, exercises are employed to clarify and justify student beliefs and personal reflections. Another common approach to teaching business ethics has been the analysis of management case studies, which provides for active dissection of ethical judgments and their fall-outs in legal, business, and cultural contexts….Another common techniques utilized in business ethics education in undergraduate and graduate business departments include offering courses that analyze the scandals of companies such as Enron, WorldCom and Health South. Avoiding the duplication of similar scandals is the goal of such pedagogy (2009, pp. 67-68).

To clean up ethics in corporations and business, one has to start at the beginning of a career, which means in most cases business schools. Bateman (1998) noted that for business schools' ethics course, "one model is a normative approach based in philosophy" (p. 48). That is, traditional ethical theories and principles, rooted in philosophy, are taught to the students, who then are shown how these ethical theories and principles can be applied to controversies to arrive at logical and rational moral decisions. Derrick and Carr (2008) ask what is the outcome or goal of learning: "Do we teach for knowledge or skill or wisdom? Or, do we teach for learners who can exhibit all three through creativity, curiosity, self-direction, problem-solving, personal responsibility and persistence in learning" (p. 18). They assert that true learning should be "shifting the emphasis from knowing and remembering to facilitating and enhancing the skills and attributes that sustain lifelong learning" (Derrick and Carr, 2008, p. 18).

In order to promote ethics education at their own school of business, The H. Wayne Huizenga School of Business and Entrepreneurship of Nova Southeastern University, and in the business community, to make ethics education morally efficacious, as well as to foster personal responsibility and life-long learning, the first two authors of this book, as Faculty Chair of Management and Lead Professor for Law and Ethics, have developed for the MBA program the required ethics course called the Legal, Ethical, and Social Values of Business. Although it is not the purpose of this book for the authors to explicate in detail the course and its components, the authors nevertheless deemed it to be useful to discuss briefly the rationales for the course, the knowledge and skills the course intends to impart, critical course elements, and how the authors hope this course will be helpful in promoting moral conduct on the part of the business students. In addition to promulgating a discrete and focused ethics course, the authors also recommend that in all the other courses in the business program the professors need to teach how ethics and social responsibility are pertinent, valuable, and value-creating.

Ethics Course Content

The ethics course is, fundamentally, a course about values. A "value," of course, is something that possesses worth; and values can be intrinsically worthwhile, that is, good in and of themselves, such as happiness, or instrumentally worthwhile, that is, good because they produce or are a means to other values, such as money (Cavico and Mujtaba, 2009). The three values in the course are: legality, based on the law; morality, based on ethics as a branch of philosophy; and social responsibility, based on a definitional principle of the term "social responsibility." Although these values are discussed in an intrinsic sense, especially the values of morality and ethics, the course also emphasizes the instrumental nature of these values, and accordingly the business students are inculcated that by adhering to these values, even if "merely" instrumentally, they, their companies and organizations, and society as a whole will benefit in the long-run. So, for example, even if a student may not believe in the truth to morality or ethics intrinsically, they are taught not to reject and discard these values, but rather to consider the instrumental worth to them and the good that can be achieved by adhering to values, even instrumentally. The course, therefore, does incorporate, appropriately so, some philosophical elements, but it is not a philosophical inquiry as to what is truly true; nor is the course a didactic, preaching, moralizing type of course; but rather the course is an exercise in applied ethical reasoning. The three core values to the course are legality, morality, and social responsibility.

Legality, of course, is based on the law, and accordingly the course covers legal principles appropriate to the graduate business student's educational and business needs. Attention is paid to government regulation of business laws since those laws, such as the field of anti-trust, were created to prevent and punish immoral conduct by businesses, such as restraints of trade. Moreover, particular attention is paid to those legal doctrines, principles, and rules which legally may permit immoral business conduct. So, for example, the exceptions to the Foreign Corrupt Practices Act are underscored, as these exceptions may legally allow "bribery" in certain circumstances. Similarly, the bona fide occupational qualification (BFOQ) exception to the Civil Rights Act is emphasized since that exception may legally permit discrimination. Furthermore, the critical legal distinctions between a legal monopoly and illegal monopolization, as well as between legally trading on inside information and illegal insider trading, are stressed. The purpose is to not only highlight those "gray" areas of the law where unethical conduct may nonetheless be legal, but also to enable the students to analyze ethically the questionable but legal practice, for example, legal "bribery," in order to see if the practice is moral.

The value of morality is based on ethics as a branch of philosophy. While the authors did not intend to convert the course into a philosophy course (and nor are they qualified to do so), nevertheless the authors firmly believe that some philosophy is appropriate for graduate level students. The moral philosophy, of course, provides the students with the ethical theories and principles that they will use to make moral determinations of business conduct as well as to ascertain if the law itself is just. As noted, the intent of the authors was not to have a preaching, moralizing, "thou shall not" type of course; rather, the authors wanted to create a graduate level course where the students reason from principles – legal and then ethical – to make legal and moral determinations. Logic, reasoning, and rationality are the key values in such a course. This type of reasoning from ethical principles, in order to logically make moral determinations, places a person at the highest level of Lawrence Kohlberg's moral cognizance-maturity-development scale. The course focused on four key ethical theories: ethical egoism, ethical relativism, Utilitarianism, and Kantian ethics based on Kant's Categorical Imperative.

Ethical egoism tells a person to advance his or her own self-interest, as that is the right, smart, and moral course of conduct to take. Yet, the students are counseled to take heed of the two major constraints of ethical egoism; that is, the true ethical egoist must take a long-term perspective of maximizing his or her own self-interest; and the true ethical egoist should not harm people, take advantage of them, exploit them, or trample on their rights, since such conduct is contrary to advancing one's self-interest in the long-run; rather the true ethical egoist will be nice to people, work with people, make them part of the "team," and co-opt them, as it is better to have friends and allies than enemies.

Ethical relativism is a societal-based ethical theory in which morality is determined by what a particular society believes is moral. Graduate students, particularly in a very heterogeneous and international locale as Southeast Florida where the authors' university is located, are certainly used to this theory, at least in practice, and consequently are prepared to relate what "has to be done to get the deal" in certain foreign countries. The authors naturally want the students to be aware of this theory as an ethical theory, and want the students to be aware of local customs, practices, and norms, but the authors also point out the limitations to this theory and the moral harm it can engender.

Utilitarianism theory is based on the writings of English philosophers Bentham and Mill. Actually, the students are used to one key aspect of this theory, that is, foreseeing and predicting and then measuring and weighing the consequences of an action, yet only as these consequences impact the students, their families, and their firms; so the authors "merely" ask the students to expand the scope of their analysis to include in their calculations of the effects of the action on other stakeholders impacted by it, including society as a whole. Although Utilitarianism is a very egalitarian ethical theory in that everyone gets "counted" since everyone feels pleasure or pain, the one major problem is that it morally legitimizes an action that causes pain or harm to the minority. Everyone gets counted, but when the counting is done, if the good consequences outweigh the bad consequences, the action is moral. Thus, the ends do justify the means, at least pursuant to this ethical theory, and so the students are taught.

Kantian ethics is based on the moral philosophy of the German philosopher, Immanuel Kant. Kant thought it reprehensible that any ethical theory could morally legitimize pain and suffering of anyone. Accordingly, Kant declared that in ethics one should disregard the consequences of the action, and rather focus on its form and ensure that the action itself, that is, the mean, passes a formal ethics test that Kant called the Categorical Imperative. Thus, the authors in the course conclude the ethics component to the course with an explication of the Categorical Imperative, which explication is beyond the purposes of this work, yet the students are instructed that even if an action produces more good than bad, it still must pass the Kingdom of Ends test, which is one part of the Categorical Imperative, and accordingly the action must treat people with dignity and respect and as worthwhile human beings and "ends" in themselves, and never as mere "means" or in a demeaning or exploitive manner. The students are asked to consider for their own lives beyond the classroom, and to treat for the purposes of the course, Kant's ethical principle as, in fact, what Kant declared it is, that is, "categorical," meaning the supreme, absolute, and universally true ethical precept.

So, in the course, the students are asked to analyze case studies first from the legal perspective, and then from the four ethical perspectives as briefly noted above, in order to determine if a particular action, for example, a pharmaceutical merger, is legal based on the law, and then moral based on the four ethical theories. The goal, the authors assert to the students, is to find an action that is of course legal, but is also moral pursuant to the four theories; that is, the action advances the self-interest of the student and his or her organization in the long-run, is one in conformity with local norms and mores, is one that produces more good than bad under Utilitarianism, and most importantly is an action that produces all this good without demeaning, disrespecting, abusing, or exploiting people so as to satisfy Kantian ethics. The authors must note that, as the reader has perhaps noted, these ethical theories are Western ones and reasoned-based ones. The reason for the Western "slant" to the ethics is due to the fact that the backgrounds and experiences of many of the professors who teach this course are Western trained and oriented. However, professors are certainly permitted and encouraged to bring in non-Western ethical theories and principles; and the students are permitted in their term papers to choose in addition to the mandatory Utilitarian model another ethical theory of their choosing. Also, if the reader recalls the discussion of religion and ethics earlier, the discerning reader will see that these ethical theories are reason-based ethics theories. The authors, at least for the core ethical elements to the course, wanted to keep religion out, and rather use reason-based ethical theories, since the authors assume that all their students possess reason, but not necessarily religion and certainly not the same religion. Yet the students are permitted to use as the additional ethical theory for their term paper and class presentation a religious-based ethical theory. Of course, since the students are using more than one ethical theory to analyze cases morally, it is quite possible that the students may come up with conflicting moral conclusions based on the types of ethical theories applied to the case. Yet the students are told that such a result is part of ethics and ethical reasoning, and there is no "supreme court of ethics," so they are just going to have to resolve their ethical conflicts, perhaps by adopting one ethical theory as "their" dominant ethical theory.

The final value to the course is social responsibility. The students are taught to consider beyond the values of legality and morality the responsibilities of business to society as a whole. The professors seek to work with the students to create a definitional principle for the key term "social responsibility"; and once such a principle is established the students apply the principle to the cases and ask themselves, and then answer, to use the previous example, what a socially responsible merged pharmaceutical company should be doing for society. The students are counseled to take a prudent and rational approach to the nature and scope of their firm's civic and charitable activities, to tie such social responsibility efforts into the firm's products, services, brand, advertising, and marketing, whenever possible, and most importantly not to "give the shop away," that is, to take primary cognizance of the shareholders or owners and other immediate stakeholders of the company. The students are firmly told that these values, particularly morality and social responsibility, are not mere academic classroom values, but rather real-world values for the students and their firms, as there is a clear societal expectation that the students and their businesses will act not only in a legal manner but also in a moral manner, and when the business is successful there is also an expectation that the firms will "give back" to the community in a socially responsible way.

The final element to the law and ethics class is to get the students to think of business management and entrepreneurship as not "mere" professional activities, but rather as emerging professions, like the established law and medicine professions. The legal and medical professions are predominantly self-governing, but they are governed by codes of ethics; members possess obligations to society as whole; the professions can be entered only by the passing of exams as to knowledge and skills and also by passing good moral character examinations; and one must take a public oath to uphold the values of the profession in order to enter the profession. Ethics, stewardship, and public and social responsibilities are hallmarks of the professions. Accordingly, the students are asked to reflect on where business management and entrepreneurship presently stand on this "professional" v. "profession" divide; and consequently what business has to do, as well as should do, to reach that elevated and autonomous "profession" status and concomitant trust, deference, and respect.

The authors, therefore, in creating their school's MBA law and ethics course, wanted to have not a mere academic exercise, but rather a practical, reason-based, graduate level educational experience, based on the law (and highlighting the moral "gaps" in the law), imparting and using ethics as a branch of philosophy, and using an agreed-upon and realistic definition of corporate social responsibility. The "drill," the content, and the skills that the authors wanted to teach is quite simple and straightforward: "Is it legal, is it moral, and what would a socially responsible firm do"? That is the essence of the graduate law and ethics course. The authors trust that such a course will enhance not only the moral awareness of the students, and improve their ability to ethically reason to moral conclusions, but also make them more moral in their personal and business lives.

Ethics Essential to Capitalism

Today there is a deepening recession and an economic crisis; and business is blamed in part, and perhaps mainly, for the banking, financial, and real estate collapse. Have business people become so consumed with the single-minded pursuit of seemingly obscene profits that the values of legality, morality, and social responsibility have been ignored or violated? Perhaps some business leaders had become so obsessed. Have they forgotten that free enterprise and capitalism cannot be conducted, they cannot survive, and consequently society cannot prosper unless business is based on a solid foundation of transparency, legality, morality, and ethics? Ethics is essential to capitalism, as there is not enough law - precise and exact and all-encompassing law, as well as lawyers and government regulators-to govern business, the markets, and the economy. Ethics, ethical standards, and moral conduct ultimately must come from, and from within, business people. Business managers, executives, entrepreneurs, and especially leaders must have a "moral compass"; that is, they must have a moral sense and ethical judgment as well as the moral character and integrity to do what they know is the right thing to do and not do what they know is wrong. They thus must self-regulate themselves; and accordingly must treat business management as a profession, like law and medicine, with enforceable codes of ethics, stewardship responsibilities and obligations to society as a whole; otherwise they are asking for even more government regulation, including even more draconian criminal laws. Schools of business, as emphasized, must take the lead in raising business to, and holding business to, the moral standards of a profession. It is also important that schools take a broader stakeholder approach and inculcate the concept of the social responsibility of business. The objectives of business schools are not "merely" to produce economically successful graduates but business leaders who will create a better society. Ultimately, for capitalism to survive and prosper, for economic growth to be restored and to flourish, and for the U.S. and global economies to be healed and functioning well once again, the commitment to morality, ethics, and social responsibility on the part of business people is never more critical.

The Moral Imperative for Business

The economic recession of the last few years did have one 'good" effect; that is, it made the world more global, made it more global in a very short and compressed time period, and made that global context very "loud and clear." Accordingly, it should be clearly aware to all, that in this "new economy," in the words of the old poem, that "no one is an island." The world economy, as was convincing and depressingly indicated, is just too interconnected for any nation to live as an island. Business schools must of course be aware of this "new reality"; and they may have to change their business models to reflect the shifting nature of markets and the economy to a global context. Accordingly, business schools now must be innovative and entrepreneurial, and be willing to take some risks, in order to take the lead to build global coalitions to produce students who will be global leaders. Due to the changing nature of the global economy and the concomitant need to take some risks and to be innovative and entrepreneurial, a business school will not be successful and may not even survive unless it "gets this." The goal, therefore, is for business schools to meet the demands of their students and to make a positive contribution to their communities, society, and the world. Business and management should be perceived like law and medicine as a "noble profession," – one that creates wealth but also brings economic vitality to their communities and society, and ultimately to transform people's lives. A commitment to ethics and a societal mission are the hallmarks of a profession; the core virtues of a profession are ethics, morality, social responsibility, duty, stewardship, and custodianship; accordingly, schools of business must underscore the importance of ethics and the broader social mission of business; they must progress from teaching mere "vocationalism," and rather must inculcate to the students the importance of creating long-term value – and not "merely" for the shareholders but for all the firm's stakeholders. Schools of business must admonish the students when it comes to short-term thinking and ethical lapses. The focus of business education should be on ethics and social responsibility and the production of sustainable growth and positive value. Schools possessing such objectives and aspiring to such "profession" status will grow, develop, flourish, and prosper with their colleges or universities, communities, and society. Of course, business as a "profession" will require an oath, that is, a public pledge, like the doctors' Hippocratic Oath or the nurses' Florence Nightingale Oath. Business students could take the oath at the graduation where they affirm that they will obey the tenets and standards of the profession, particularly the commitment to legal, ethical, moral, and socially responsible conduct. Dean Angel Cabrera, dean of the Instituto de Empressa business school in Madrid, Spain, suggests the following oath for business students: "I will utilize natural resources in an efficient, sustainable way. I will respect the rights and dignity of the individuals working for the enterprise. I will engage in honest and transparent transactions. If I do not violate this oath, may I enjoy life and art and personal success. May I be respected while I live and remembered with affection thereafter" (Alsop, 2003).

Summary

Business schools and ultimately business students naturally will make business decisions, yet such decisions must be balanced by the needs of the school's and society's stakeholder groups. The administration, faculty, and students must "buy into" the school's mission, vision, and core values principles; and then they all will want to make their "mark," a positive mark, in higher education, business, and society, and grow and prosper with their schools, communities, society, and the world. Business schools should be leaders in bringing forth not "merely" economic growth and vitality but also moral and socially responsible behavior; and thus business schools should, and must, produce business leaders who can effectuate positive, value-maximizing, sustainable, and successful change on a global basis.

Chapter 4

Accountability, Responsibility, and Governance

Educating tomorrow's business leaders requires teaching business students the critical concepts of legality, morality, and ethics, and also the notions of social responsibility and corporate governance. The purposes of this chapter[3] are first to enumerate and explain various types or levels of moral accountability. Then the chapter will examine the topic of the social responsibility of business. The chapter next will analyze the subject matter of corporate governance, taking a broad approach that encompasses legal aspects, especially government regulation of business, as well as ethical and social responsibility components. The chapter, finally, will again raise and address the topic of business management as being construed as more than "merely" professional but as a profession, and concomitantly what exactly such "profession" status entails. The goal is for business schools to teach the students how to be good, how to do good for themselves, their organizations, communities and society as a whole, as well as to how to be successful and sustainable business leaders, managers, and entrepreneurs.

Introduction

In order to address social responsibility, it is first necessary to examine moral responsibility, and then to distinguish moral

---

[3] For more information on this chapter, see Cavico, F. J. and Mujtaba, B. G. (2009). *Business Ethics: the Moral Foundation of Leadership, Management, and Entrepreneurship*. Pearson Custom Publishing: Boston, United States.

responsibility from legal responsibility. It is critical for a school of business to differentiate among these key concepts when creating and teaching a law and ethics class. A person is accountable casually for all the consequences of his or her actions, regardless of intent, volition, or the length and attenuation of the causation chain of events. A person, for example, is responsible casually for the actions he or she does while sleeping, or for striking a child who jumps in front of his or her car, or for an ultimate, remote consequence produced in an unusual manner by an attenuated causation chain. It is important to note, however, that even though a person casually may be accountable, he or she neither may be legally nor morally responsible. A person is responsible legally for his or her intentional, wrongful actions, and careless, negligent, wrongful actions, as well as the foreseeable consequences thereof. Such legal liability is deemed misfeasance or malfeasance, and is legally actionable. Nonfeasance or not acting, however, ordinarily is not legally actionable. As a general rule, there is no legal duty to act (only to act carefully when in fact one does choose to act), and thus no legal liability for not acting. Consequently, a person who has not caused another's peril, or who is not in any "special relationship" with the "victim," is not under any legal duty to rescue or to come to the "victim's" aid; such a person is not liable legally for not acting and failing to help the person in need. A strong swimmer, for example, does not commit a legal wrong by refusing to rescue a drowning victim.

Moral Accountability

When is a person morally responsible or accountable for having performed an action? A person is responsible morally for an action he or she knowingly and freely performed or brought about; he or she is responsible immorally when the act was morally wrong to be performed or brought about. A person also is morally responsible for the reasonably foreseeable consequences of such an action. Although one acts immorally, there may be circumstances that exonerate one's moral responsibility. Moral responsibility may be excused or lessened because of the actor's ignorance, inability, or lack of freedom. Certain circumstances tend to eliminate or to lessen the required knowledge element to moral accountability. Moral responsibility is excused if the necessary knowledge element is missing completely, and it is mitigated if knowledge is less than completely present. Moral responsibility may be lessened, or even eliminated completely, if one is ignorant of the relevant facts. A person cannot be held accountable morally for failing to meet an obligation of whose existence one was legitimately ignorant. One may be ignorant of the circumstances giving rise to a particular obligation, or one may lack knowledge of the consequences of an action, although one is deemed accountable for the reasonably foreseeable consequences of an action. One also may be ignorant because one fails to recognize the existence of moral reasons or relevant moral standards that one ought to have recognized. Ignorance, however, does not always excuse a person. One, for example, cannot claim justifiable ignorance when one purposefully chooses not to ascertain the relevant facts, circumstances, or moral standards. One also cannot use ignorance as an excuse if one carelessly fails to become informed; that is, if one could have, and should have, known of the relevant facts, circumstances, and standards. Moral accountability concerns actions that are in a person's power. Accordingly, one morally is not responsible for performing an action that is an impossible action for one to perform. If one lacks the ability, skill, opportunity, or resources to act, one is relieved of moral responsibility. If, for example, one does not know how to swim, one cannot be held responsible morally for letting someone drown (if swimming is the only way to save); or if one is driving carefully, and a child jumps in front of one's car, making it impossible for one to stop in time, one is not responsible morally for hitting the child. Moral responsibility does not exist without freedom of action. There may be internal or external circumstances that render a person unable to do, or unable to keep from doing, something. An action is not free when one is subject to compulsion, constraint, duress, lack of control, or lack of alternatives. An internal, irresistible, internal compulsion may arise within a person, for example, a kleptomaniac, that removes moral responsibility. One may lack control, for example, for actions done in one's sleep, or when one faints and knocks over a lamp and starts a fire. One may be subject to external force or coercion that eliminates or lessens moral responsibility. The validity of such a defense depends on the nature and degree of the threats, for example, a threat of death or physical harm, as opposed to an employer ordering an employee to falsify a report or else be discharged. Therefore, performing an immoral action, or failing to perform a moral action, without a recognized excuse reflects poorly on one's moral character. One may be condemned as morally weak or stupid when one can act, should act, and yet one fails to act on the facts and reasons that one knows, or ought to know, one should be acting on.

When does one have a positive moral obligation to act? Acting morally may involve more than merely avoiding negative harm; acting morally also may require one to perform an affirmative positive action, even though legally one may not be required to take the action. The ethical principle of "last resort" indicates when one has a moral duty to act, to aid another, or to rescue. One morally must act when there is a need, proximity, capability, one is the last resort or chance to avoid the peril, and when acting would not cause harm, or threaten to cause harm, equal to or greater than the original peril. The principle is based partially on Kant's admonition that "ought implies can," that is, that one is obligated to do only what one can do. Thus, if one is unable to act and help, due to lack of opportunity, means, or resources, one is not obligated morally to act. The "last resort" principle usually involves an obligation of immediacy and high priority posed by an emergency; it thus generates a moral obligation to act that one cannot ignore without moral condemnation. The classic example is a drowning case when the five "last resort" factors are present. The problem in successfully applying the "last resort" principle to business, however, emerges the fourth and fifth factors. Who is the last resort for people unemployed and in need, business or government? Would business "rescuing" in fact harm the corporation, or its shareholders, or other stakeholders? A "friendly takeover," a corporation helping an employee pay his or her children's college tuition, may be praiseworthy actions, but are they morally required under the "last resort" principle? Is a corporation immoral for choosing not to act in the preceding circumstances? Again, it is critical for a school of business in the teaching of a business ethics course to ask, and with the students seek to answer, this question.

Social Responsibility

Although business may not have a moral responsibility, based on the principle of "last resort," to improve the quality of life in the community and society, business may be obligated by a standard of social responsibility to work for social as well as economic betterment. A corporation, as well as a person, can have a non-moral duty, the failure to perform, which is not a moral wrong; yet one can be held accountable for failure to perform a social obligation. The words "accountability" and "responsibility," of course, imply some sort of an obligation on the part of business to deal with social problems. "Obligation" suggests that society may demand that business act in certain socially responsible ways; otherwise, perhaps, society will compel business by law to fulfill its social obligations.

What exactly is a corporation's "social responsibility"? Does a corporation have a social obligation to take care of the poor, educate the public, give to charity, and fund cultural programs? Again, these are key questions that a business ethics course must address and seek to answer. Social projects and social welfare traditionally have been viewed as the appropriate domain of government, not of business. Business, of course, is taxed and such taxes may be used for social purposes. The traditional purpose of business, moreover, is the profitable production and distribution of goods and services, not social welfare. Yet by raising the issue of social responsibility, business is forced to concern itself with the "social" dimension of its activities.

What is a definition of this "social responsibility?" The term may be defined as taking an active part in the social causes and civic life of one's community and society. Where, however, are the corresponding guidelines for corporate contributions? How should a corporation's resources be allocated, and exactly to whom, to what extent, and in what priorities? A corporation, of course, exists in a competitive environment and thus is limited in its ability to solve the multitude of social problems. If a corporation unilaterally or too generously engages in social betterment, it may place itself at a disadvantage compared to other less socially responsible business entities. Being socially responsible costs money, and such efforts cut into profits. In a highly competitive market system, corporations that are too socially responsible may lessen their attractiveness to investors or simply may price themselves out of the market. There is a further problem in expecting the corporation to take on the betterment of the "general welfare." Corporations already possess great power, and corporate executives neither are the elected representatives of the people nor are answerable directly to the general public. Corporate executives lack the mandate that a democratic society grants to those who are supposed to promote the general welfare. Government officials, elected by the people, rightfully are thought of as the social guardians of the people.

Social responsibility, however, at least to some reasonable degree, may be in the long-term self-interest of business. The authors believe, and have always believed, that the value of social responsibility should be given an egoistic justification in a business school ethics course. A corporation cannot long remain a viable economic entity in a society that is uneven, unstable, and deteriorating. It makes good business sense for a corporation to devote some of its resources to social betterment projects. To operate efficiently, for example, business needs educated and skilled employees. Education and training, therefore, should be of paramount interest to business leaders. A corporation, for example, can act socially responsible by providing computers to community schools and by releasing employees on company time to furnish the training.

Business also gains an improved public image by being socially responsible. An enhanced social image should attract more customers and investors and thus provide positive benefit for the firm. A corporation that acts more socially responsible not only secures public favor, but also avoids public disfavor. Business is part of society and subject to society's mandates; and if society wants more "responsibility" from business, business cannot ignore this "request" without the risk of incurring society's anger, perhaps in the form of higher taxes or more onerous government regulation.

The social responsibility of business has been heightened by the creation of social responsibility investment funds which promises to invest the participants' funds only in companies that are ethical, moral, and socially responsible. Naturally, investors want to invest in quality companies whose business will make a profit for the shareholder-investors; yet socially responsible investors want to invest in such companies only if they also are sensitive to the needs of other stakeholders, and conduct business in an environmentally responsible manner. Today, many socially responsible funds exist, including mutual funds; and the socially-minded investor has a wide choice of funds, ranging from those that stress environmental causes and workers' rights, to those that reflect ethical and religious values.

Above and beyond the responsibility to act legally and morally is this notion of social responsibility. The law defines legal accountability; ethics determines moral accountability, but ascertaining the nature and extent of social responsibility emerges as an even more challenging task. Nevertheless, there exist today several "socially responsible" investment firms to ensure investors they are investing in not only financially prudent companies, but socially responsible ones. So too must the students in a business ethics course determine what exactly "social responsibility" means in a business context and what criteria are to be used to determine if a company is a socially responsible one.

Although there is an outcry, and admittedly a righteous one, that business should be socially responsible, one problem that has emerged is the permissible degree of pressure that a business can exert on its own employees to be socially responsible, especially when the demands entail the employee to spend his or her own money or personal time in charitable and civic-minded activities. Is it moral to pressure employees to be socially responsible? This is an issue too that the authors feel must be addressed in a business ethics course. The good to the community might very well outweigh the "pain" in the form of expense and effort to the employees, and thus such "coercion" might be moral pursuant to Utilitarian ethics; but is the employee being treated as a mere "means" or instrument by his or her employer; and although for good ends, is the employee being so demeaned so as to make the employer's pressure immoral pursuant to Kantian ethics. Of course, if the employer is allowing its employees to be socially responsible on the company's time by encouraging them to participate in employer-sponsored volunteer programs, there should be no moral problem. Yet forcing employees to be socially responsible in addition to their work demands and workday duties can equate to unpaid and thus unethical overtime. Some employers will require such "volunteer" work, track the employees' time and efforts, and even assign the employee "volunteer" points on his or her performance evaluations. At the least, the employer should allow the employee, who very well may be very busy with a home life and personal commitments, to write a check to a charity as opposed to physically serving in a civic capacity. A better and more moral option, since it is not coercive, would be for the employer to have a released-time program, for example, a "charity day," in which the employees would be released from work to volunteer for certain approved charities. The employees would have some flexibility in choosing their volunteer projects, and, most importantly, the employees would be paid by the company for their charity work. Such a program would naturally benefit charity, treat the employees with respect, and, despite the expense, would benefit the employer in an ethically egoistic sense in the long-run.

The topic of social responsibility has emerged as such a critical one for global business and for business schools that the World Bank now has an Internet course on social responsibility, called "CSR and Sustainable Competitiveness," offered by its educational and training division, the World Bank Institute. The corporate social responsibility course is designed for "high-level" private sector managers, government officials and regulators, practitioners, academics, and journalists. One major purpose of the course is to provide a "conceptual framework" for improving the business environment to support social responsibility efforts and practices by corporations and business. The course is also designed to assist companies to formulate a social responsibility strategy based on "integrity and sound values" as well as one with a long-term perspective. By being socially responsible, declares the World Bank, businesses not only will accrue benefits, but also civil society as a whole will benefit from the "positive contributions" of business to society.

Corporate Governance

The term "corporate governance" is a broad one, encompassing in the business context the legal, especially the government regulation of business, moral and ethical, and social responsibilities of the business. Most people think of corporate governance as having a predominantly legal foundation; and certainly the legal aspects of such governance are significant; yet all the aforementioned critical components to the subject matter of corporate governance must be covered in any proper examination of this area. Large, publicly-held, state-created, multinational business corporations, administered by professional managers, dominate modern economies. They are the center of the capitalistic system, the instruments of production and service, the basic source of income and wealth, and a major source of government revenues. They help make the "good life" possible, yet these corporate entities raise significant legal, moral, and social responsibility issues globally. Consequently, these corporations are a primary target for those people and groups who condemn the immorality of business, particularly in the "developing world." Corporate managers, therefore, must be prepared to confront and to resolve legal, moral, and social responsibility challenges. Since legal, moral, and social responsibility problems are important and unavoidable, any efficacious approach to business ethics must pay special attention to the role and function of large business corporations. This section accordingly reviews the legal and moral status and social responsibility of the corporation, which today is known as "corporate governance."

The legal status of the corporation is a critical initial corporate governance issue to address. A corporation is a special kind of entity; it is a "creature" of law, an artificial legal being. The corporation is created by government, in the United States by state government. No one can conduct business as a corporation without a grant or franchise from the state. States generally have promulgated corporate statutes for business corporations, nonprofit corporations, professional corporations, and small, "closely held" corporations. State statutes, moreover, regulate in detail the formation and activities of the corporation. State statutes vary, although most are patterned on a uniform, "model," business corporation act developed by commercial and legal experts. In most states, a corporation is formed by filing the appropriate document, usually the Articles of Incorporation, with the appropriate state official, usually the Secretary of State, and paying the appropriate fee. Corporate existence is deemed to begin on the date of filing as indorsed on the document. The appropriate state official, the secretary of state or perhaps the attorney general, is charged with primary responsibility for administering corporate laws. A corporation is an artificial legal entity, independent of its owners, the investors, created by the state, pursuant to a corporate charter, with powers conferred upon it by the law, and subject to the law. A corporation is regarded as a separate legal entity, that is, an artificial person, distinct from its shareholders. The corporation is owned by its shareholders, but overall policy is determined by a board of directors chosen by the shareholders; and day-to-day management is implemented by officers chosen by the board of directors as well as employees and agents selected by top management. A corporation can conduct business in its own name, much in the same way as a natural person does. Assets can be acquired, contracts entered into, and debts incurred, all in the name of the corporation. The corporate entity can sue and be sued, pay taxes, obtain a business license, purchase real estate, and own a bank account, all in its own name. A major feature of the corporation, as well as a primary reason for its creation, is the limited liability of the shareholders, who are not personally and unlimitedly liable for corporate obligations beyond the extent of the shareholder's investment. The ethical justification for limited liability usually appears as a utilitarian one. The limited liability encourages the formation of corporate business, and thus the doctrine produces greater benefits for society, such as providing remunerative work for members of society, producing goods and services for social use, paying taxes for governmental and societal needs, and generating investment capital for economic development and growth. As a general rule, the shareholders are only limitedly liable; their liability is limited to their investment; they are not personally liable for corporate obligations. An important exception, however, arises from "piercing the corporate veil" doctrine. If the law determines that the corporate entity is being abused or misused, the corporate entity can be disregarded and the shareholders held unlimitedly and personally liable for the organization's obligations. This exception arises when the corporation is being used to defraud, to avoid a valid obligation, to evade a statute, or when corporate separateness ceases to exist and the corporation becomes a mere shell, instrumentality, or alter ego of the principals involved. It is important to note, however, that the mere fact that the primary motive for incorporation is to secure limited liability is not enough in and of itself to trigger the "piercing" doctrine. Since a corporation is an artificial person, it acts exclusively by and through officers, employees, and agents. Thus, agency and employment law is very important in the corporate setting, but beyond the scope of this book. A moral problem does arise however, when the corporation's agents or employees commit a criminal act on behalf of the corporation. It is obvious that the corporation itself cannot be sent to prison, even though the corporation is a "person" legally. The corporation, of course, can be fined when it violates criminal statutes. Imposing a fine on a corporation for its criminality raises interesting and important moral, legal, and practical issues as to whether fines are sufficient to punish and deter corporate misbehavior. If criminal conduct, however, can be attributed beyond a reasonable doubt to corporate officers, employees, and agents, these individuals, as natural persons, may be held liable criminally and imprisoned for their actions.

The Constitution of the United States guarantees a "person" certain protections, and a corporation is treated as a "person" for most constitutional purposes. The corporation, for example, is entitled to the First Amendment's freedom of speech guarantee. "Pure" speech, that is, political expression, is fully protected. Commercial speech, that is, advertising proposing commercial transactions, is accorded lesser legal protection. Since the motivation behind commercial speech is predominantly economic, government is allowed to regulate commercial speech, even legitimate and truthful commercial speech, if there is a substantial government interest in regulating the speech and government does so in a direct and narrow manner. The dividing line between "political" or public affairs speech and "mere" commercial speech is a difficult one to demarcate. The corporation also is treated as a person for full protection under the Fourteenth Amendment's "equal protection" and "due process" guarantees, the Fourth Amendment's guarantee against unreasonable searches and seizures, and the Fifth Amendment's "double jeopardy" guarantee. The corporation, however, does not possess the Fifth Amendment's privilege against self-incrimination, although the corporation's officers, employees, and agents, as natural people, do possess the right. A corporation, therefore, is a legal person, a person under the law, and protected by most of the same rights as a real person. As the corporation is a legal entity and legal actor, and since the law treats corporations the same as individuals in most respects, the important issue arises as to whether a corporation is similarly a moral entity and a moral actor, and thus subject to ethical analysis.

The next important and related corporate governance area to address is the moral status of the corporation. Moral responsibility usually is ascribed to and assumed by individuals. What about the corporation? Is it a moral entity and a moral actor? Is the corporation subject to ethical analysis? Can it be accountable morally for its actions, or does moral accountability only make sense when applied to the human components of the legal entity? This chapter seeks to answer these questions and to ascertain what "moral responsibility" means when referring to corporations.

A conventional view of corporate accountability, advanced principally by Milton Friedman, University of Chicago economist and Nobel prize-winner, holds that the corporation is not a moral entity. At most, it is a legal entity, which is bound by the law and legally accountable. Human beings, however, are not only legally accountable; they also are moral actors subject to moral accountability. The corporation, the artificial legal person, therefore, is not a moral actor; it has no moral responsibility and it should not be evaluated ethically. The "business of business" is to make money. Moral, as well as social, responsibilities are not the proper concern of the corporation. Successful performance in the marketplace and increasing profits are "right" corporate conduct. Assuming there is any moral or social responsibility for business, it is met in terms of marketplace performance. Accordingly, there is no need to consider a corporation's moral or social responsibility other than perhaps successful economic performance, within the law, of course. Another version of the Friedman or organizational view maintains that formal organizations, such as a corporation, do not act; rather, the human beings therein act, make choices, and perform whatever the organization needs to do. The organization itself is nothing more than a structure, perhaps a legal one. It does not make choices, act purposefully, or on its own volition. It only acts through the human beings who compose the corporate workforce. Since the formal organization does not act, this view holds that it is not subject to ethical evaluation. Many arguments are advanced against the Friedman or Organizational view. Ethics governs the actions of rational actors when they have an effect on people. Corporations act rationally pursuant to rational, hierarchical, decision-making processes and structures. Corporations possess reasons for what they do. These rational actions, in addition, have an impact on people. Corporate actions, therefore, can be evaluated ethically from a moral perspective. Otherwise, the potential exists for moral abuse and exploitation, because actions by a human being may be branded as morally wrong, yet the very same actions by a corporation, perhaps even a closely held or even one-person corporation are neutral and morally unaccountable. If, for example, it is deemed immoral for a person to discriminate, then it should also be immoral for a corporation to discriminate. If it is wrong for people to steal, it should also be wrong for business to steal.

Corporate actions, of course, do originate and flow from the choices and actions of human beings. These real people, moreover, are morally accountable for these actions. Yet, these actions and choices are not merely personal ones; they are made for and in the name of the corporation. People within the corporation are acting on behalf of the corporation and not strictly for themselves. Since the corporation is controlled by human beings who initiate and implement corporate actions, the corporation possesses a moral status that makes the corporation subject to ethical analysis, even though the corporation may not be a moral "person" per se. There are practical advantages, in addition, by holding the corporation morally accountable. Ethically evaluating corporate action and making moral judgments enable one to attach praise or blame to corporate actions. If a corporation is deemed to be a moral actor, one can exert moral pressure within or on the organization to rectify a wrong, change a policy, or implement an action. For example, the cessation of the use of plastic packaging by fast-food restaurants, the marketing of condensed milk as a substitute for mother's milk in the developing world, and the use of dolphin-friendly tuna nets are corporate activities that changed in response to moral pressure.

Any focus on the corporation as a moral entity must not ignore or obscure individual moral accountability. When moral accountability is ascribed to the corporation as an entity, responsibility also must be assumed by the human components of the organization. One cannot allow the corporate fiction to act as a shield to hide the individuals who underlie the entity and who are the ultimate and primary bearers of moral responsibility. The corporation and also the people within it have moral status. It is a moral agent, though not necessarily a moral "person." The corporation, therefore, can be held responsible morally for its actions and inaction, as well as legally responsible. In particular, the corporation is bound by the basic ethical duty not to inflict moral harm on others.

Since it is postulated that the corporation does indeed owe moral obligations, the next area to examine is exactly to whom these responsibilities are owed. The current interpretation of business ethics reflects a broadening of the corporation's responsibility beyond the law into the realm of ethics, which results in moral responsibility. Assuming that the corporation is a moral actor, the question arises as to whom the corporation owes moral duties, particularly the duty to do no moral harm. The conventional view was that the shareholders as the "owners" of the corporation were the only real stakeholder group and thus the board of directors and officers had, and only had, a legal duty to examine the consequences of corporate actions on the shareholders. Today, however, in order to encourage, and perhaps legalize, board attention on other stakeholder groups, most states in the United States have adopted statutes, called corporation "constituency" laws, that allow (but do not mandate) that the board consider the consequences of corporate decision-making on other stakeholders, including the local community and society as a whole.

The principal constituent groups or stakeholders to whom the corporation owes moral duties are: shareholders, employees, customers, consumers, suppliers, the community (local and national), society (in general), and even the competition. All these groups are owed the same general ethical duty to do no moral harm, as well as specific duties due to the nature of the group. A difficult problem arises, however, when the corporation's obligations to one group are perceived as harming another group. In any discussion of corporate moral obligations, shareholders usually are addressed first. Obviously, the corporation cannot survive if it does not serve its shareholders well. Shareholders are entitled to honest and efficient management of their investment as well as a fair return on their investment. A corporation that abuses its shareholders, for example, by paying extraordinary pay and bonuses for merely ordinary executive performance or worse, cannot expect to exist, let alone prosper, in the long run. A problem arises, however, when the corporation's effort to fulfill its moral obligation to other stakeholder groups is perceived as limiting the profitability of the corporation and ultimately harming the shareholders. The corporation is morally responsible to its employees. It is immoral for the corporation to ignore the needs of its employees as human beings. Employees, accordingly, are entitled to fair employment practices, a just wage, reasonable job security, safe and healthful working conditions, and privacy from immoral employer intrusions. The corporation's moral obligation to the consumers is to produce goods that are morally safe, to provide services that are competent, to avoid deceptive practices in advertising and marketing its products and services, to provide consumers with adequate information regarding the goods and services, and to refrain from immoral and anticompetitive trade practices. What moral obligation does the corporation owe the local community? Generally, the corporation owes a duty to this constituent group to do no moral harm. It is important here to distinguish the corporation's moral duties, based on ethics, from its social responsibilities, such as supporting nonprofit organizations and enterprises in the community. One area that a corporation's moral obligation to the community may rise is the closing of plants. This is not to say that ethically a plant can never be closed morally. Ethics will impose a duty on the corporation, however, not to forget the community's contribution to the development of the plant and to its operation. A minimal moral obligation requires the corporation to minimize the harm the corporation's closing of the plant will inflict on the community, as well as the corporation's own employees. Another corporate obligation involving the community involves the corporation's obligation not to harm the environment, and, in particular, not to pollute the air and water beyond morally acceptable levels. What is the corporation's moral duty to society at large, to the wider social community, the state, nation, world, and even to unborn generations? The general ethical obligation, of course, is to do no moral harm; accordingly, one must use an ethical decision-making process to determine specific obligations, such as not to exploit developing nations, nor to exploit resources needed by future generations. The corporation, finally, has a moral obligation to its competitors not to harm them by immoral means, to prevail by superior merit and not by immoral tactics such as making questionable payments that distort the marketplace and by other abusive and predatory practices. In order to determine the extent and nature of the moral obligation owed to stakeholders Wal-Mart now has a new corporate position, Senior Director of Stakeholder Engagement, whose job is to help the company create value for all its stakeholders, including society as a whole.

Moral responsibility, moreover, is not only attributed to a corporation, but also to people within the firm who compose the company, in particular, directors, shareholders, managers, and employees. Directors are morally responsible for the "culture" or tone of the corporation and for its major policies. Directors are accountable morally for the decisions they make, and fail to make, especially the selection of honest, competent, and moral managers. Directors are responsible morally for overseeing management and for ensuring that the longer-term interests of the shareholders are looked after. In so doing, as noted, the directors may take into consideration the consequences of corporate actions on the firm's other stakeholder groups, including society as a whole, and may do so on a long-term basis. Today, in the post-Enron, intensified legal and ethical environment, assuming the role of a corporate director definitely emerges as a more daunting challenge for the concerned businessperson. Instead of honing one's golf skills, and then after a perfunctory review, merely "rubber-stamping" a CEO's policies, directors are now learning the complexities of corporate governance and financial accounting; and are being compelled to very closely examine the actions and performance of the company and its executives. The new era of responsibility was dramatically marked by the promulgation in the U.S. of the federal Sarbanes-Oxley law in 2002, which significantly increased criminal penalties for corporate fraud. Moreover, as a consequence of the Enron corporate scandals, directors were made well aware that they could be sued civilly, and personally be held liable, for the harm that resulted from their failure to fulfill their duties as directors. In addition to legal scrutiny, shareholder "activist" groups are now closely examining directors' actions regarding the compensation packages of company executives, especially "golden parachutes," which many angry shareholders have condemned as frequently so excessive and unrelated to performance so as to be unethical, even if technically legal. Directors are now in the "spotlight," and accordingly are being forced to "go back to school" to learn corporate legal, business, and accounting subject matters (and perhaps a seminar or two on ethics would be a very good idea too!). Directors also now must ask corporate executives and managers difficult, pointed, probing, and even embarrassing questions, as well as closely monitor their conduct. Directors now also must meet as a board much more frequently, particularly the audit and compensation committees of the board. Meeting eight times a year as a board and also monthly for the aforementioned committees is rapidly becoming the corporate norm. The result of the heightened scrutiny of directors, the additional work burdens, and the increased risk of legal liability – civil and criminal – is that many business people no longer find the "job" of being a director an attractive and beneficial business option. For example, regarding executive compensation, new rules promulgated by the Securities and Exchange Commission now require that directors not only disclose the true extent, whether salary, bonus, stock option, severance, pension, etc., as well as detailed nature of, executive compensation packages, but also explain how and why they decided to pay executives such compensation. Serving as a board member today, therefore, is certainly a more challenging endeavor; yet better educated, more involved, and better informed board members, particularly those who take a leadership role, surely should help to ensure legal as well as ethical business behavior. Managers are responsible morally for keeping the directors fully informed of actions and decisions made and contemplated and the financial condition of the firm. Executives are responsible for implementing the business policies set by the board, for administering the day-to-day affairs of the company, and for selecting and supervising "top" management. Managers are accountable for selecting honest, competent, and moral employees and for "running" the company on a daily basis. In a small or closely held corporation, the shareholders generally are the directors, executives, and managers, and thus directly are accountable morally for the corporation's actions. In a large publicly held corporation, a shareholder normally represents a very small ownership stake. He or she is separate from management and possesses no direct voice in the affairs of the corporation, only the right to vote for directors and fundamental changes pursuant to his or her proportionate shares. Nonetheless, even a small shareholder can be held accountable morally for what a large corporation does or fails to do. If a corporation acts immorally, for example, and a shareholder becomes aware of such actions, he or she is obligated morally to attempt to change corporate policy, and if not, to sell his or her stock. Focusing on shareholder rights and responsibilities, therefore, emerges as a central element to corporate governance. Jacobs (2009) asserts that business schools cover the subject of corporate governance by focusing on two principal areas: 1) the board of directors, including board structure, composition, and processes, particularly how the compensation of board members should be effectuated; and 2) shareholders, including the rights and obligations of shareholders and how a shareholder-based corporate accountability system can function properly. These areas, obviously, are necessary for any examination of corporate governance. The authors, though, take a broader perspective of corporate governance, and thus view the concept as one that incorporates legal, ethical, moral, and social responsibility conditions and requirements to the operation, management, and control of the business entity.

Yet one can take an even more expansive perspective. When judging people, it is appropriate to determine their integrity and moral character. What about the larger issue of a corporation's integrity? Does a corporation have a moral character? These are also corporate governance issues. A corporation can be said to possess a moral character if it takes its moral responsibility seriously and continuously and seeks to act morally in its dealings with its stakeholders. Corporate moral character, as with people, is built by the regular past and present performance of moral actions. As a result of such actions, acting morally becomes habitual and a tradition of morality arises. People composing the company take pride in their moral company. They identify with the moral history and tradition of the company. They adopt the company's moral stance, seek to continue the tradition, and help educate and mold others to the moral corporate culture of the firm. A company, of course, can have a corporate culture that inhibits, as well as fosters, moral conduct on the part of its members. Some firms may have a strong positive moral corporate culture, yet others may evidence a negative approach, or no approach at all, to moral concerns. The role of directors and management is essential in ensuring a rightful moral culture. Corporate culture initially is formed by, and constantly is sensitive to, the decisions of management. Management establishes the direction that the company follows. Management can act morally and can insist on morality throughout the company, especially on the part of the employees. Managers can set the moral pattern, eventually developing into a tradition of moral action on the part of the corporation and its employees, producing a company with a deserved reputation for moral excellence.

Moral accountability and corporate governance also entail codes of ethics. An ethical code should serve human needs; it should treat people as they are and as they can be expected to become. A code cannot demand conduct beyond the capacity of ordinary people in ordinary circumstances. An overly idealistic and thus unattainable code results in noncompliance and engenders a general breakdown in morality. An efficacious code, therefore, differentiates fundamental moral rules to do no moral harm, which should be simply set forth and binding on all, from the higher levels of conduct, exemplified by saints and heroes. Distinguishing levels of conduct is extremely important when one attempts to hold people accountable and to exert moral pressure in the form of praise and blame. It is permissible to pressure a person to carry out a basic moral duty, such as promise-keeping, and to hold that person morally accountable for failing to comply with that duty. It is, however, highly objectionable to pressure a person to perform an act of saintliness or heroism. It would be outrageous, for example, to pressure morally a person to sacrifice his or her life for others. Saints and heroes, however, do play a worldly role. They can be used to demonstrate virtues that are worth admiring and to a degree emulating and thus they can help people learn how to live a moral life.

It is also important to differentiate levels of accountability when making demands and exerting pressure on business. There are three legitimate types of demands that can be made against a corporation. Legally, a corporation must obey the law and is held accountable for breaking the law. A corporation also is morally accountable. Morality, of course, stems from ethical principles. The essence of a corporation's moral obligation is to do no moral harm. Moral obligations, moreover, remain whether or not enacted into law and whether or not socially mandated. It is necessary to recall that a corporation does not have a moral obligation to do good, that is, to engage in "good works" and social causes, unless the ethical principle of "last resort" is applicable. What about social responsibility, that is taking an active part in social causes and charities and the civic life of the community? A corporation should be involved socially to a limited degree, and a corporation must be cognizant of the fact that society can impose on business certain social obligations that are neither legal (at least initially) nor moral.

Role responsibility, agent responsibility, and collective responsibility are also key components to corporate governance. Role responsibility encompasses assuming a certain position, role, or occupation in society or in an organization, or by becoming a member of a certain profession. These roles usually impose responsibilities that have a moral dimension. A parent, for example, has a moral obligation to sustain and nurture his or her child, a corporate executive has a moral obligation to be an honest and efficient manager for the benefit of the shareholders, and an attorney has a moral obligation to represent zealously the interests of his or her client. Members of a profession frequently assume special moral obligations inherent in the profession, for example, a duty of altruism when a physician or attorney undertakes pro bono work. When a member of a profession assumes a role in an organization, he or she carries a role responsibility of the profession in addition to the role responsibility stemming from his or her organizational role. This dual role responsibility poses a potential problem for a corporate employee who is also a member of a profession. Loyalty to the corporation may conflict with responsibility to one's profession. In weighing the conflicting role responsibilities, the duty to one's profession should prevail, as the professions are grounded on codes of ethics. When one assumes a position in a business as an employee, one takes on the responsibility of performing the functions of that role and obeying the rules of the employer. Normally, when one follows the rules and performs the work functions, one fulfills his or her obligations to the employer. Following the rules and doing one's job, moreover, is an acceptable explanation when one is called to account for one's actions. However, if an organizational rule or employer order requires one to act immorally, merely "following orders" or "obeying" the rules is not an acceptable response and does not exonerate those who hold the roles and follow the rules and orders. Role responsibility is subordinate to general moral responsibility, as determined by ethical principles. Business people, therefore, must be careful and avoid adopting a "role morality" mentality, which may cause them to abandon their ethics in the belief that the sacrifice is necessary to succeed in a highly competitive environment. In performing the functions involved in one's employment role, it often is thought necessary, convenient, customary, or otherwise expeditious to compromise one's ethics in order to "get the job done." The challenge for an ethical person is to resist the temptation to sacrifice ethical principles to expediency, and still be successful. Clearly, it must be understood that business objectives, and even profession status, do not supersede fundamental ethical principles.

The subject of agent responsibility is a difficult corporate governance one – legally, morally, and practically. A large organization, such as a corporation, usually reflects a hierarchical structure of authority, where orders and directives emanate from those higher in the organization to a variety of subordinates, or agents, at lower levels, who act on the basis of orders from their superiors. Such an organizational structure at times raises problems of moral accountability. For example, who is morally responsible, and to what degree, when a superior orders a subordinate to carry out an immoral act? One view holds that the subordinate even though he or she was the agent in the immoral act's execution nonetheless is absolved from responsibility and consequently only the superior is accountable. It is wrong, however, to exonerate totally a subordinate or an employee for example, who knowingly performs an immoral act on the grounds that he or she was merely "following orders." The superior, of course, morally is held accountable because he or she knowingly and freely brought about the immoral act through the means or agency of the subordinate. The fact that the superior used a human being as the instrument does not alter the fact that the superior brought about the immoral act. Subordinates, moreover, even those at the bottom of the hierarchical chain, remain moral agents and cannot deny moral responsibility for their actions. There is a limit to a subordinate's role responsibility to obey the order of a superior: one is not under an obligation to obey an order that is immoral, and thus the subordinate is morally responsible for carrying out the immoral act. However, because subordinates may make an arguable case that they were "forced" to do what they on their own would not freely choose to do, their moral responsibility may be diminished.

The subject of collective responsibility has always been a very challenging area, and not just in the business realm. Assigning or assuming moral accountability within an organization raises the issue of collective responsibility. In a corporation, for example, the actions of the artificial legal "person" are brought about by real people and typically brought about by the joint actions or inaction of many people. Within the corporation, therefore, moral responsibility may be distributed among a number of cooperating participants in the organization, as well as the entity itself. The question thus emerges: who exactly is morally responsible for the corporation's actions? Legally, the acts of the corporation generally are attributed to the entity, so long as the board of directors, managers, agents, and employees act with authority and within the scope of their authority. The notion of collective moral accountability, however, is ambiguous and may be interpreted in a variety of ways. The "individual responsibility" view holds that those people who knowingly and freely did what was necessary to produce the corporate act are each morally accountable. The "group responsibility" view holds that when a group of people, such as a corporate "group," jointly acts to produce a result, the act is the act of the group, and thus the corporate "group" and not the individuals who compose the group is morally responsible. The "legal" view of collective moral accountability attributes responsibility to the entity itself and not to the people involved either as individuals or as a group. Neither the "legal" nor "group" theory alone is valid interpretation of the moral accountability involved because neither accurately reflects the moral reality behind the entity's actions. People, as individuals, had to formulate and execute the particular actions of the impersonal entity. Individuals, therefore, are responsible morally for the known, intended, and foreseeable consequences of their freely chosen actions and also for joining their actions with others to produce a group result. The fact that action is deemed that of the entity, or that group decision making was involved, does not operate as a shield to deflect legitimate moral accountability. Moral accountability is attributed to the entity, the group, as well as to the individuals involved.

Management as a Profession

In any discussion of business or management ethics and corporate governance, it is necessary to differentiate "mere" professionals from members of a profession, to determine a manager's place in these classifications, and to understand the ramifications of a manager as a member of the "management profession." These objectives as previously noted should be key features of any business school's business ethics course. Business, of course, is inextricably and extensively linked with professionals and members of the professions. As society and business have become more complex and specialized, requiring distinctive knowledge and skills and advanced training and education, more people and groups attempt to identify themselves as professionals and as members of a profession. Serious ethical considerations, however, are raised by the use of the terms "professional" and "profession." A great deal of confusion, moreover, exists between the two terms. It first is essential to grasp a fundamental point- that all members of a profession are professionals, but not all professionals are members of a profession. Many people who are professionals, therefore, are not members of a profession. Professionals are people who work on a full-time basis, for "high" pay, and who possess considerable skill, expertise, and knowledge. Professionals have undergone specialized, systematic, and required training and learning. They are self-supervisory, tend to set their own tasks, often do not "punch" time clocks, and work as many hours as are required to do the job, often at inconvenient times. Professionals, accordingly, possess status and rank in society. Members of the skilled trades, such as electricians and plumbers, commonly are regarded as professionals, so too are people who engage in "professional" activities, such as actors and athletes. These trade and professional activities, however, do not constitute professions. Members of a profession are professionals who meet certain "profession" characteristics. They command prestige and respect. They have attained a superior reputation and great influence arising from their success and achievements. Members of a profession are admired and esteemed. They have advanced education and are subject to mandatory continuing education. The professions are autonomous; they are self-governing, self-regulating, and, in essence, are state-authorized monopolies. Members of the profession control and regulate entry into the profession, set the standards and policy for licensure (which entails not only a skills and knowledge evaluation but also a moral character analysis), set the standards for practice, police the profession, and discipline and discharge members who do not live up to the profession's standards. Why does society permit the professions to possess so much power, power that it denies to "mere" professionals and to business managers? The professions are accorded such power because society requires such people to possess specialized knowledge that is clearly useful to society, but society requires proof that these people have mastered such knowledge, and are qualified to practice, and that the members of the profession are practicing in a competent and proper manner. Another very important reason for granting autonomy to the professions is that the professions set higher moral standards for themselves than society sets for other people and groups, including professionals and business managers. These higher moral standards, moreover, are embodied in the codes of ethics of the professions.

Members of a profession are bound by its code of ethics. If the profession's code is a legitimate code, that is, one that can serve as the basis upon which the profession rightfully can claim autonomy, the code must set standards beyond self-interest and beyond the law. The code must set as standards higher moral norms. These norms must serve society and not merely the members of the profession. Members of the profession are expected to adhere to these higher moral standards, and they risk sanctions and discipline, including the ultimate penalty of expulsion from the profession, for engaging in unethical conduct. "Professional" organizations and associations, in addition to their education and information functions, promulgate and enforce the ethical codes of conduct of the professions. Being a member of a profession also involves the taking of an oath, which is a public admission of the moral obligations assumed. It is most interesting and revealing to note that the deans of several business schools have proposed that business school graduates take an oath in which they pledge to be morally upright and socially responsible managers. Such an oath would certainly enhance the "profession" status of "mere" business "professionals."

When one enters into a profession, one enters into a fiduciary relationship. A member of a society is compelled to rely on and trust a member of the profession, and a member of the profession can be trusted to serve interests other than the member's own. The member of the profession is expected to use his or her power, knowledge, and skills for the benefit of society. The professions are service-oriented and not merely profit-oriented. Members of a profession are not simply sellers of expert, specialized services in the marketplace. The obligation a member of the profession undertakes to the profession, and ultimately to society, may require a degree of altruism and effacement of self-interest on the part of the member, which at times may be detrimental to the member's own economic self-interest. The trust and confidence and altruistic aspects of the professions, as well as the code of ethics involved, stand out as critical differences between members of the profession and "mere" professionals and business managers.

The two traditional occupations that are regarded as the best representatives of the professions are the medical and legal professions. Doctors and lawyers are bound by codes of ethics. They must adhere to the higher moral norms set by the profession. Doctors, for example, are required to treat people even if they cannot pay; lawyers likewise are required to defend people even if they cannot pay. Craft and tradespersons, however, even if deemed "professionals," as well as business managers, are not expected to work without pay. In addition to doctors and lawyers, other examples of the professions are accounting, pharmacy, engineering, architecture, and nursing.

Business managers certainly are professionals, but they are not yet members of a profession. Why would management want to be regarded as a profession? Professions traditionally carry with them great prestige, respect, and especially autonomy. Society permits the professions a large degree of autonomy- power that it denies to business managers- and members of a profession function with far fewer restraints than do business managers. In return for the right to govern themselves as a profession, members of the profession must serve society, set higher standards of conduct for themselves, formalize these standards in codes of ethics, and enforce these standards by disciplinary measures. Business managers may desire the attributes of profession status, but are they willing to undertake the special, heightened, and sustained moral responsibilities? Managers must be aware that morally and socially, more will be expected and demanded of them when they become members of the "business management profession"; and the benefits that accrue to members of the management profession are legitimate only to the extent that managers conform to its higher moral code. What if the Business Management Code of Ethics demands conduct on the part of a manager that conflict with the loyalty and obedience expected by a corporate employer? Will the manager obey the higher standard set forth in the code? Is the "management profession" ultimately serving the public and promoting the public good; if so, how? The development of a code of ethics is the key factor in transforming management from "professional" to "profession" status. A code of ethically developed moral rules can act as a guide for the practice of the Management Profession, and it can serve as a link among academia, management, business, and the well-being of society. Discussion of the creation and implementation of such codes as well as the examination of current business codes of ethics must be an integral part of a business ethics course.

Summary
Moral accountability, social responsibility, and corporate governance are indispensable for successful and "sustainable" business education and for business, and thus these values, in addition to legality and ethics, are moral imperatives for all individuals, especially business leaders and educators who aspire to business management as a noble profession. Even, and perhaps especially, the Pope, Benedict XVI,

called for a new world business order guided by ethics and social responsibility and the search for the common good. In the third encyclical of his Pontificate, called, "Charity in Truth," the Pope condemned business for having a profit-at-all cost business mentality and consequently causing the current global recession. The Pope firmly stated that the world economy needs ethics in order to function correctly and well, and that the ethics must be people-centered. Therefore, the imperatives for business and government leaders, the Pope declared, are to produce a financially viable and sustainable future and to create a more socially just society (Winfield, 2009). The current economic crisis certainly has raised some "cautionary tales" as well as produced some "hard lessons" for business people and business schools. The most important are to persistently teach and to steadfastly adhere to the values of legality, morality and ethics, and social responsibility. Corporate governance, accordingly, means not "merely" obeying the law, but also acting in a moral and ethical manner when the law is absent or unclear, as well as acting for the long-term goal of benefitting society. Governance, therefore, means not governance just from and by laws and legal bodies, but self-governance, in the mode of a profession, by means of ethical principles, moral rules, and socially responsible conduct.

Chapter 5

Training and Development

The quality of a school's education and the school's graduates is likely to be heavily influenced by the knowledge, skills, and credentials of their faculty, administration, and staff. Therefore, developing and training faculty members to integrate unique delivery methods, updated knowledge, and innovative technology into the classroom for student learning are basic necessities in today's competitive world of education; but many educators fear or resist change due to lack of effective training and development. As such, administrators should focus on the effective development, training, and retaining of qualified educators to teach in various learning modalities (online, on-ground, and "blended" formats), using "cyberspace" technology while focusing on effectively achieving learning outcomes. Administrators must ask for participation and interaction of experienced educators in order to glean and highlight their successes as well as to confront the challenges they now face in serving the needs of diverse student populations in distance education. Both the means and processes for effective faculty development and training, on a just-in-time basis with the least cost, should be implemented by the administration.[4]

Introduction

Many traditional and non-traditional universities have integrated online education into their delivery systems to enhance their offerings and student learning (Mujtaba and Preziosi, 2006). Schools must

---

[4] For more information on this chapter, see the original source: B. G. Mujtaba and R. Preziosi (2006). *Adult Education in Academia: Recruiting and Retaining Extraordinary Facilitators of Learning* (2nd edition). Information Age Publishing: United States.

develop standardized training programs to make sure their faculty members are trained and developed, and are successfully using cyberspace technologies as they compete to survive, and also hopefully to capture a segment of the market share in education using online modalities. Peter Drucker, the "father" of modern management, maintained that universities will not survive if they do not adjust to distance learning. Perhaps it is true that the future is outside the traditional classrooms and the traditional campuses. Training and development programs may vary in terms of skill and pedagogy, but many schools are creating programs that use online training as their basis, due to its low cost and flexibility of scheduling, in educating qualified faculty members and students throughout the globe so long as they have access to the Internet. Distance education and distance learning are realities of life, and educators should embrace it in order to create a healthy learning environment for diverse students. Educators must use distance education technology to enhance their offerings. However, they also need continuous training and development opportunities to keep up with the changes in the application of technology.

Developing and educating faculty members are today's necessities, as new technology to enhance learning is being introduced rapidly, so everyone can stay updated and skilled in their usage. A major element of effectively assisting faculty members to develop is to understand the nature of how adults learn best, and then create an environment and the processes that are conducive to learning effectively. Some administrators may be of the mindset that educators are already developed, and consequently they learn by osmosis; as such, they do not require formal development. A colleague in the corporate training world used to say that "people learn differently and facilitators of education are people too." Faculty members, just like other adults, need to be involved in the learning process in order for the learning to be enjoyable, effective, and long-term oriented. Just-in-time education, learner participation during the session, and interaction are critical to effective facilitation techniques that increase learning and retention with adult learners. A major element of being, or becoming, an effective educator involves understanding how each group of participants learns best, and then integrating activities that best suit their learning styles regardless of teaching modality. Adults are autonomous, self-directed, goal-oriented, relevancy-oriented, and practical, since they tend to focus on the aspects of a lesson most useful to them in their work. Furthermore, they have accumulated a foundation of life experiences and knowledge that may include work-related activities, family responsibilities, and previous education. An effective facilitator must remember that, as do all learners, adults need to be shown respect.

While considering the aforementioned characteristics of adult learners, facilitators should acknowledge the wealth of experiences that adults bring with them that can be integrated into the learning modules. These adults should be encouraged to take initiative in their learning, and they must become a part of the learning process through effective facilitation by the facilitator and appropriate administrative processes that allow learners to become a part of the learning experience. There are many elements that should be considered with adults in the educational environment; and one is that adults are likely to engage in learning activities before, after, or even during any challenges facing them (which are described as "teaching moments" or "teaching opportunities"), and they are likely to engage in learning that promises to help them cope with the transition. Furthermore, adults are concerned about their self-esteem and ego, which influence their behavior. Facilitation should respect their dignity and self-esteem concerns. Facilitators must remember that the average adult can effectively focus on a limited number of concepts at a given time. The facilitator or trainer, therefore, should effectively balance the presentation of new material, discussions, sharing of relevant experiences, and the time allotted. Trainers and facilitators should recognize that adults want their learning to be problem-oriented, personalized, and appropriate to their need for direction and personal responsibility.

Learning and Facilitating

Learning is about the enhancement of one's capacity for effective action both immediately and in the near future. Learning is about building knowledge that brings more joy and opportunities to make better and more valuable contributions to one's field, industry, profession, and society. Knowledge is not just the ownership of information, but rather knowledge is one's capacity for effective actions; and the more immediate the need for relevant action the greater the need for learning. Human beings are designed to learn by nature. Each person has the natural drive, capacity, and "hunger" to learn. People have the capacity to create the kinds of jobs they want to be in as well as to create the types of communities and societies in which they want to live. Unfortunately, many ineffective training and development sessions at many institutions do not encourage this freedom because they are, and have always been, very "controlling." Top officials think, and lower level employees act, as has been done in most traditional or centralized organizations. Traditionally in schools, educators lectured, and learners memorized, to the best of their abilities in order to reproduce correct answers on the examination. This system has not been very effective for society, and it certainly will not be very effective for adult learners who teach others. Accordingly, facilitators must work with each individual faculty or groups of faculty members to effectively develop them in the appropriate and timely use of advanced technology in the achievement of course learning outcomes with extraordinary results.

Mahatma Gandhi once said that one should "*Learn as if you will live forever, live as if you will die tomorrow.*" Extraordinary teachers continuously learn and pass on relevant and current information to their students. Michael Jordan, the extraordinarily successful basketball star, said "You have to expect things of yourself before you can do them." The same can be applied to faculty members' teaching styles and expectations as they assess or reflect upon their own performance in the class, and also expect and strive for higher levels of success with their students in achieving the stated learning outcomes by becoming extraordinary teachers and learners.

Online Education and Pedagogy

Faculty members wishing to teach online should become online students first, and thus learn the pedagogy of online education along with the school's electronic platform. This immersion model of training has been used to train corporate trainers and to develop faculty members in distance education. Understanding its practical application, successes, challenges, and "best practices" can be of great assistance as a starting place. Some suggestions offered for beginning online faculty members are:

- Learn and understand the mechanics of how the online environment of education works.
- Collect best practices and tips for beginning online faculty members to be effective in their initial online experience.
- Discover what learning strategies work best for teaching and learning the course material.
- Know how to best engage students, keep them interested and "on track" to achieve course and curriculum learning outcomes.
- Learn how to best manage time to adequately show presence on the discussion board. The minimum number of times faculty members should log on to their courses each week must be clarified for a foundational standard and consistency.
- Find out how to best manage discussion threads with large quantities of comments.

There are many "best practices" that new online faculty members can absorb, perhaps through osmosis, and benefit from, as they observe an actual class facilitated by an experienced online educator. Furthermore, online administrators and facilitators should discuss and integrate some or all of the following suggestions for online courses:

- Use the basic technology available to everyone in the market; and the sophistication of technology requirements should be kept simple or to the lowest common denominator.
- Software, content links, and "self help" training sessions should be regularly updated and made available asynchronously. Technical support experts should be available for online learners and educators seven days a week, and 24 hours each day, as online education is about learning at one's own pace and time.
- Ask for contributions from faculty members, staff, and students on ways to improve the system. Involve everyone that is impacted by the process, hear their concerns, and, when possible, integrate their suggestions.
- Rules, policies, and training material should be formal and standardized. However, the training and facilitation of the content should be personalized, to the extent possible, based on learning styles and the individual needs of each learner.

- For best results and when possible, effectively and appropriately use both asynchronous and synchronous formats depending on the learning objectives. Because adults like to learn at their own pace and time, synchronized online learning and assessment requirements should be limited to the bare necessities when used.
- Communicate regularly with online faculty members and students about the technology usage, software updates, and overall program objectives. Also, questions submitted through emails and bulletin board postings should be answered within a 24-hour period or as determined by the needs of learners and the availability of resources.
- Create a standardized mechanism for documentation of "feedback" and development for each learner. This helps the faculty member to effectively observe, monitor, evaluate, and develop the progress of each learner. Similarly, such a process can greatly assist the learner understand his/her "learning gap," and as a result to do what is possible to close the gap between where he/she is and where he/she intends to go at the end of each term or module.
- Compensate facilitators fairly while considering the amount of work that goes into preparing for the class, "interaction" time, content preparation, time while the class is in session (asynchronously or synchronously), and communication time or follow-up needed with learners once the session has ended.
- Periodically measure and assess the actual learning to make sure it matches the intended learning objectives. Online groups can be compared with each other or with groups that meet face-to-face, learning the same content through similar facilitation. Statistical analysis can be performed for data over time, and relevant conclusions can be drawn. Make appropriate adjustments as needed.

Cyberspace Education

Pedagogy in online education requires the application of learning techniques and facilitation that work in the on-ground environment using different mediums or modalities of delivery. For example, students take tests to show their understanding of the concepts, theories, cause and effect relationships, etc. to the faculty and the institution. In the traditional classroom, students can complete their exams using a computer, the paper and pencil format and/or through oral examinations. Online faculty members can do the same things using online mediums both asynchronously and synchronously, by using proctored formats when needed. Computerized cameras and teleconferencing technology have made the impossible possible and yesterday's vision into today' reality for online students and faculty.

For effective learning of students, online faculty members should be involved in class interactions each week (four-five days per week) and respond to questions within 24-48 hours, especially since the new generations of learners are being conditioned to expect "feedback" instantly through the widespread use of "instant messaging," "twittering," "Face-book" postings, and other such communication devices. If one is not able to adhere to such simple guidelines by providing "feedback" to students in a timely manner due to other responsibilities, then one should not teach in the online modality. Online classes should achieve the same outcome as on-ground courses using online modality. Often students will spend more time on online courses than they do at the on-ground courses because there is no face-to-face interaction. Generally speaking, online courses have more assignments submitted than on-ground courses. This also means more work for the faculty. Online education is, and should be, convenient (as is the case with evening and weekend programs), but educators should not be lenient with academic rigor. The following are some general guidelines and "best practices" for online educators:

- All assignments should be posted with clear directions, expectations, and due dates. The evaluation methodology should be mentioned to students as well.
- Post a comprehensive lecture each week for students the day before the week starts. The lectures should be related to the assigned readings and the faculty member's personal experiences and thoughts about the material. The lecture should not just summarize the assigned textbook and article readings, but it should offer more examples and personal experience with the literature. Faculty members may supplement weekly lecture with PowerPoint slides and links to relevant online articles,

websites, and newsgroups. One should make sure students know that they are to read their assigned textbook readings, since faculty lectures typically are supplementary material to reinforce and/or enhance their learning.

- Discussion Boards should be monitored every other day (if not every day) and used by the faculty member in all classes. Faculty members should post and respond to students' postings regularly to monitor learning, guide interactions toward course objectives, to show presence, and to encourage effective participation. Furthermore, faculty members should post appropriate cases and topics to reinforce the weekly assignments and objectives when needed and appropriate. One should be involved and post something related to the weekly objectives of the class at least four to five days each week to raise student contributions, interest in the content and learning. One can post relevant weekly questions, dilemmas, problems, cases, etc. to achieve the stated objectives of the course and to involve students in the interaction each week.

- Holding synchronized chat sessions is a good idea to either clarify content or to test everyone's comprehension of material on a real time basis. For example, some schools encourage each online faculty to hold several chat sessions during the term with students and require students to attend at least two or three of the assigned chat sessions by awarding points (which can be a small portion of the participation grade). Attendance to two or three chat sessions should be mandatory; attendance to the remaining chat sessions should be encouraged by linking them to awarding of weekly participation points. Chat sessions can be about one hour, and they should be conducted at reasonable times to accommodate working adults. Determine chat session times and dates during the first week of class to accommodate as many of the students' schedules as possible. Chat sessions should not be confused with online office hours, since effective chat sessions can be used to evaluate students' comprehension of the material by asking them direct questions related to the content of each week's objectives. Yet, having online office hours is a good idea too in order to answer any questions for students. Online office hours often range from 10-15 minutes at a specified time each week (or day) in case students have questions about course content, assignments, or team activities.

- Presence of the faculty and requesting relevant contributions from students to specific assignments (discussion questions, case studies, article summaries, debates, etc.) each week will increase participation, interaction, student reflection, the quality of learning in each class, and the program's effectiveness. Again, the faculty member should be involved with the students each week in the online class, and at least four to five days each week, to facilitate the learning objectives.

- Quality "feedback" for all assignments should be provided to students within one week of original assignment due date (or submission), if not earlier. Timely and quality "feedback" is critical to student learning and progressive improvement.

- Participation, "feedback," and grades should be given each week (if grades are awarded on a weekly basis) or at mid-term and final week (if participation points are cumulative). If student grades are low because of lack of participation in the online classroom and nothing was communicated to them in a timely manner, then they would not be aware that they needed to improve. So, proper "feedback" in a timely manner must be provided to students starting at the end of week one of the course!

- Individual email correspondence should be reserved for personal student issues and course "feedback." All other course related discussions should be conducted in the course newsgroup and/or course bulletin board.

- Deadlines and submission policies must be consistently applied and enforced to all students. All assignments must be received by the course deadline and grades should be awarded appropriately. Offering students extended time to complete assignments without a very good reason (that is exceptional circumstances) is not a good practice in the online world either. Students need to discipline themselves to complete their work on time. Also, providing extra-credit opportunities for students may not be a good practice as it conditions some of them to not worry about completing quality assignments in a structured manner, which is very important for all students, especially in the online environment.

An important aspect of online education is the effective evaluation and "feedback" process that is ongoing for both students and faculty members. Online faculty members, especially those who are just starting to teach online, need quality "feedback" in order for them to improve their facilitation skills.

Learning Styles

Understanding one's natural or best learning style and trying to adapt other effective learning styles are necessities toward good and quick learning for time-impoverished working adults that are going to school either in the evenings, weekends, or online. A discussion with regards to understanding and becoming familiarized with online teacher's lecture style should be explored. So, the question is: how do students get used to and/or familiar with another person's style in the on-line world of education? Yes, most students will tend to have the same kind of online platform, syllabus outline, weekly discussions, and similar grading criteria for most of their courses in the program. However, the faculty members vary, and that by itself will make everything else different. Some schools do have a standardized process to make the format easier for online students. This is not necessarily the case in all schools, especially schools catering to traditional students, since some schools provide much more freedom for faculty to determine what works best for his or her classes. In those cases, the student has much work each term to get used to new styles, new requirements, and new technologies. While there may be much consistency in online programs, some faculty members are very advanced in online education/protocols, and may very well be using advanced cyberspace technologies to enhance the learning process. So, in such cases, students will have to be able to adjust quickly to new methods. So, the challenge still remains, how do students bridge the on-line style gap between one instructor and the next in their progression of classes toward graduation?

This is a very good question; and thus getting to know the faculty is critical to successfully completing assignments. One suggestion would be to get to know the faculty's syllabus and then see how he or she approaches the learning outcomes each week through lectures and assigned readings (students can see the faculty's first week lecture and compare with learning objectives for the first week of the course). In some courses, faculty members may put more stock on students reading the assigned textbooks/articles and some of their lectures will be short and to the point since each course may have one or more specific textbook(s) for that topic. In other courses, textbooks are tools that can and should be used throughout the course and research process, but faculty members may provide more detailed lectures or articles for weekly readings.

For the past decade, online services have been conquering the education and training market "like there is no tomorrow," and consequently one sees that consumers all over the world are "throwing themselves" over their keyboards. Why? Customer service is best delivered face-to-face; otherwise it seems to be a bit mechanical or automated, but then again it is all about convenience. What this means is that communication has its routes and forms; adaptation on the other hand is only a matter of time. Ascertaining the style in writings can never be simple in accordance to the time span of electronics that we have been encountering lately. In the case of online students, communicating with an online instructor and getting to know him or her without seeing the person, and what he or she has to deliver, all depends in his or her words and the way of typing them and, most importantly, how fast the words can penetrate to thoughts, rather than merely telling or dictating to students!

Online students should quickly condition themselves to the platform used by the cyber faculty and adjust to the teacher's requirements. This is very similar to the on-ground platform; however, online modality may be new to many adult students and they do not yet have the requisite experience with it. As such, faculty members should do what they can to familiarize students with the requirements at the outset of each course. This can eliminate much undue stress, frustration, and negative student-faculty evaluations which are traditionally completed toward the end of each course by students.

Many schools have switched the student evaluation of the course and faculty procedures to the online format because of its convenience and timely processing for improvement. The purpose of this new system is to create a "paperless" student-faculty evaluation process that can be forwarded to faculty members as soon as their course grades are submitted. Also, administrators can take the necessary steps in improving the service for students if needed and appropriate. Oftentimes, administrators send emails to both faculty and students so they can complete the online evaluations. The student completion rate of course evaluation through the university's website or online links usually seems to be much lower than on-ground courses. If one is like most faculty members, one wants the "feedback" from students, because it helps improve or change teaching techniques to enhance the overall goal which is learning. There are other benefits besides improving one's teaching style or techniques. Evaluations help administrators with merit promotions for full-time faculty, and they may increase the opportunities to teach more classes for part-time faculty. Furthermore, and more importantly, good "feedback" keeps everyone in touch with the learning environment and the learners by providing timely responses and replies.

Faculty Training

The adult world of education, using blended formats of distance learning delivery, has achieved a special market in the adult world by offering quality educational programs, both nationally and internationally at times convenient to students. Through professional faculty members committed to student learning and their ability to combine academic theory with successful practical tools, as well as their ability to effectively adjust to the changing educational needs of working professionals, online educators have and can offer great value to their students and the community at large. Accordingly, many schools have enjoyed increased enrollment over the past decades due to their quality, convenience, and satisfied stakeholders.

No matter the program or format, each program should utilize all the tools technology and management have to offer, giving students an unprecedented opportunity to acquire information and skills that will enrich their "knowledge base" and enhance their leadership abilities, while learning to add value to their company and to their lives.

The following, therefore, are some general recommendations for administrators and program directors of various centers and/or schools that wish to replicate this Faculty Training and Orientation process in their departments:

- Create an experienced committee made up of faculty, staff, and administrators to design, prepare and implement the faculty training and orientation program. The leaders and senior faculty members must continuously support and nourish the program. Not many things can exist productively for very long without periodic quality nourishments. So, the leaders have to "plant the seed," provide sufficient nourishments for it, and then watch it grow.

- One of the first things that must be done by the pertinent committee and faculty members is to create a complete list of course profiles and qualification requirements for all courses in the program. Then, educate everyone on how this document can be used to recruit the right persons for teaching the courses. As such, the faculty coordinators and program managers must be thoroughly educated in the process so they can be empowered to use and improve it.

- Clarify and communicate the program's vision, expectations, and orientation process to all faculty members and administrative staff so they can both support and promote it.

- Schedule at least one faculty assessment and orientation session each quarter, or as needed, so the new faculty members can be "indoctrinated" to the school's culture on a just-in-time basis for teaching in the upcoming semesters (as per the school or college's needs).

- Once the sessions are scheduled, each program should review its projected (or actual) enrollment for the coming few terms to assess their faculty hiring needs. Then the appropriate administrator of faculty member can select resumes for interviewing.

- Interview qualified candidates and invite those who match the school's needs to the assessment session.

- Conduct the assessment and orientation session for all newly hired faculty members.

- Once the candidate's hiring paperwork and orientation session are successfully completed then schedule a course for this faculty in the coming term and assign a mentor to work with this person.

- Follow up to make sure the person is ready to teach his/her first course. Offer any assistance that the candidate or the mentor needs.
- Once the newly hired faculty member's class is over, speak with the mentor and the newly hired faculty to assess the success of the new faculty.
- All faculty members should be given "feedback" on their performance on a regular basis. It might be best to implement a formal and standardized program where each faculty goes through a peer review process annually. Corporate and government employees often receive a formal appraisal each year, and the same should be true of academics as everyone can use quality "feedback" to set goals and improve their performance.
- Learn from the experience, improve the orientation program, and continue this process each term or year as needed.

It is also important to mention that an effective faculty training and orientation program qualitatively involves relevant staff, faculty, advisors, administrators, and students. Furthermore, the success of this process requires commitment and resources to effectively compensate mentors and lead faculty members for developing newly hired educators. As part of service requirement to the university, it might be fair to expect full-time faculty members who are not involved on other committees to mentor two new individuals each year. When mentoring more than two mentees in a given year, full-time faculty members should be compensated fairly or given some sort of a reduction in teaching load as appropriate. It is important to note that mentoring requires work, and its long-term success depends on appropriate rewards and recognitions for all relevant parties. When resources are available, and to fairly reward each person's commitment, it is recommended that new faculty members should be given a stipend for successfully going through the assessment and orientation process. This stipend should be paid, along with the contracted compensation for the course, once the person finishes teaching his or her first course. Furthermore, it is recommended that mentors (lead faculty, full-time faculty, or senior part-time faculty members) be fairly compensated for working with each mentee as they teach their first course at the university. In such a case, when mentors are given a stipend, then they should also be required to physically observe the new faculty in the class for a period of two hours on the first session, and then once again for another two hours during the term as appropriate. Each mentor should also complete formal evaluation forms that need to be submitted to the program office for documentation and processing. When the new faculty member is assigned to teach an online class, the mentor should observe and monitor all interactions (in the background without students being aware) while providing regular "feedback" on the performance of the faculty. Of course, the specific amounts of compensation, reward, and recognition may vary depending on the teaching load or student numbers in each course, compensation for each course, contact hours with students, benefits offered, and other such variables. So, each program should discuss and design strategies that are appropriate for the program and faculty. Furthermore, the program directors should design effective documentation strategies for properly monitoring progress and performance, while continuously improving the process as needed.

The program directors and administrative leaders must also reward and recognize the assistance and contributions of everyone making the process successful. Some means of rewarding everyone for their contributions can include taking them and their significant others to a dinner, a play, or a theme park for a day or two as per their preference. Sometimes, the entire team along with one or two family members can be taken to places like Disney World, Epcot Center, Universal Studios, Sea World, or Busch Gardens where everyone can enjoy the day with each other because of their hard work and synergy as a team. This effort can be a fun and a great way of further developing cohesive groups and creating loyalty, while increasing the probability of effective communication among diverse team members and groups.

Summary

Global trends towards the removal of cultural, geographic, social, and economic boundaries are providing endless options and opportunities to individuals worldwide. The field of academia is fast catching up in this regard. Various forms of distance education, including the phenomenon of the "virtual classroom," are now being explored and expanded. New challenges are presented by these developments, both for educational institutions and their various stakeholders.

Distance education provides one opportunity for institutions to compete effectively in the global marketplace. However, structured training and orientation approaches must be developed and maintained in order to achieve success. Participants in this new era of distance education have many factors to consider, including: cross-cultural challenges; the availability of the various infrastructural support systems; and the hiring, training, development, compensation, and retention of the human resources (i.e. faculty members) who are needed to facilitate this development. Additionally, the needs of students, as well as the organizations that will be "purchasing" faculty skills, must be considered. Advances in technology have to be monitored and incorporated into the education system in order for universities to remain relevant and continue to produce graduates that enter into, fit, and excel in a rapidly changing corporate world, which today is characterized by economic downturns, fierce competition, disappearing global boundaries, and advancing information technology. Accordingly, this chapter presented an "immersion model" for faculty training and orientation that can prepare new faculty members for successfully facilitating the learning objectives of each course and curriculum in the program.

Chapter 6

Imperatives for Modern Leaders

Market leaders are innovators and creative thinkers who constantly improve their structural processes and outcomes. They think and plan "ahead of the game" and understand the requirements for surviving in a highly competitive, information-knowledge-based, and service-led globally interconnected economy. They know how and when to search for the next opportunity, implement the best alternative, and when to develop and implement new strategies. Market leaders are "drivers" of innovation, change, flexibility, and adaptability. Market leaders are environmentally responsive to the degree where they set the tone for change by being initiators and founders whether it is in the application of new technology or development of new goods and services. This is the type of leadership that 21st century and future business schools demand; leadership that is able to meet the challenges of competition and uncertainty by swift adaptability and value-creating knowledge and ideas. Today's market leaders in education must go beyond being "merely" inspirational to creating ideas that can be operational and value-maximizing from the outset.

Introduction

There is no doubt that we have been experiencing a modern leadership crisis; and this crisis does not stem from quantity but quality issues. While we have countless individuals designated as leaders or acting in capacity of leaders, there is a "famine" of truly highly effective leaders of the spirit and caliber that today's complex environment and dynamic organizations require. One of the most discouraging areas in which highly effective leadership is lacking is in the business school. This is discouraging and a serious problem, since the business school is where many organizational and corporate leaders are produced and where the mass of ideas, principles, theories, and knowledge concerning leaders and leadership practices are gained today. Whether individuals enter business schools to pursue a Master of Business Administration, Master of Science in Management, Master in International Business, Public Administration, or related field, or any undergraduate or doctoral degrees in business, management, and administration, there is certainly much discussion or theorizing on leadership, especially the ideology of effective leadership concordant with the need for success in the corporate and competitive market world.

In business schools, there is leadership at every level that mirrors society as a micro-model system. Thus, the principles and ideas concerning leadership practices are not only initiated here, but also tested within the exercise of the deanship, directorship, chairship, and professorship, among other levels of leadership that contribute to the business school's success as an organization and training and development institution for leaders. In this light, the authors have discussed several considerations, problems, and challenges, including dealing with issues of accreditation, scholarship, competition, social responsibility, morally effective leadership, strategic focus, and planning for the future by change management and knowledge management philosophies. These represent imperatives for successful leadership in business schools as well as any other modern organization. It is not unfair or overwhelming to expect and demand that business schools become and remain the models of successful leadership for the private and public sectors and the "corporate world." Many business schools use the great-leader centered approach in teaching effective leadership to their students; yet many in the process fail to demonstrate how powerful the ideas of vision and innovation are in implementing change and successfully managing it to set the tone for market transition. The business school is the most effective model for leadership in the external corporate realm because of the structure and levels of leadership present within its walls, housing a paradox of intermingling and interdependent, yet separable, leadership domains. This leadership ideally refers to the divisional faculties of administrative leadership, educational leadership, and business leadership.

Imperatives for Administrative Leaders

The success of 21st century business schools begins with having effective administrative leaders. Central to successful administrative leadership in business schools are deans and associate deans. These are the top administrative officers who must chart a direction for the school in terms of mission and vision development, strategic direction, and competitive strategy. These top administrative leaders are often accompanied and assisted by an entourage of leaders, including assistant deans, directors, and even department chairs, who are semi-autonomous administrative leaders since they are sometimes responsible for extremely large organizational sub-units or departments. The dean is the central administrative leader who must be a visionary model as well as a moral leader, especially in today's globally competitive business education "industry," where the line between the corporate and educational worlds has been erased. Business schools in the 21st century are significantly different from their predecessors when it comes to this level of leadership. Whereas in the past the focus was on academics, today's deans, while required to have superior academic qualifications and standing, must also have superior industry leadership experience, a successful business track record, corporate recognition, and strategic-knowledge of industry and economy.

The selection of a dean in 21st century business schools is a careful process that limits the position to the most accomplished and knowledgeable in the academic and corporate world. The stress on the corporate domain takes significance over academia in many cases, as business schools search for the competitive edge through image branding by known "gurus" or the industry "tycoons." These corporate deans may not have had any significant or outstanding academic publications, which in the past would have been extremely critical to any deanship. However, they are illustrative of the emerging trend of business school deanship criteria: industry notability through private or public leadership, and a very good "track record" in the business world.

The significance of the above business domain brings to realization that administrative leadership in 21st century business schools involves institutional brand-imaging, and thus demands individuals that have amassed great practical experience and networking success that can create alliance and strategic partnership networks for growth and competitive survival. Thus, administrative leadership of 21st century business schools is a mission-critical strategic approach geared toward building leadership examples and using experience and know-how to further expand training and acquisition of new and greater opportunities to stave off, survive, or beat the competition. Ideally, administrative leadership for 21st century business schools requires experienced real-world leaders with above average standing and recognition in either the private or public sector; and this is a trend that is being built upon by many institutions. While the dean is an administrative leader firstly by virtue of the changed nature of business school requisite success, academic or educational leadership is an equally significant domain. The dean must be able to understand the requirements and process of academic systems in order to be an effective and efficient administrative leader. The dean and associate dean and others in administration at the business school must also be business leaders, recognizing that the business school is an important contributor to market production, transaction, and consumption. Thus, they must lead the organization not only ethically but also with financial effectiveness and efficiency.

Imperatives for Educational Leaders

Business schools depend highly on successful educational leaders. The chief educational leader in the business school must always be the dean. The deanship, though it has taken on less academic characteristics than in the past, is still a position with great expectations as to educational direction and vision. The dean as the chief administrator along with his or her "second," the associate dean, must have significant educational background and qualifications, and that is why many business schools in the 21st century will still insist on a doctoral degree as one of the significant requirements for the deanship. This is especially the case in those 21st century business schools still holding some traditional conceptions of the nature and process of school leadership as essentially an academic rather than a business process. Educational leadership ensures that standards and quality issues related to teaching and learning, training, and development are sustained and improved. These include acquiring and maintaining essential programmatic accreditation, such as AACSB or IACBE, and membership in academic organizations and forums.

Effective educational leadership is also important for building competitive advantage through quality image. Professors are the most important groups in ensuring effective educational leadership in 21st century business schools through their abilities to "make or break" the teaching and learning process. Under the direction and motivation of a dean, who is both an effective administrative and educational-academic leader, business school professors and directors are able to develop quality programs and services for their students who are the future business leaders. Professors must possess the relevant knowledge and qualifications, industry experience, and the understanding to develop students who are aware of the complex global and volatile world in which individuals, groups, and markets operate. Collectively, leadership in business schools requires effective knowledge management; and this process is an educational endeavor. Knowledge must be strategically organized into program structures, program offerings, and curricula that constitute successful educational outcomes seen in degree conferrals, graduate success rates, and customer and shareholder satisfaction.

Educational leadership in 21st century business schools has taken on some depressing turns, which contemporary deans and their associate administrative and educational leaders must be mindful of at all times. There has been a steady decline in the rigor of programs, as competition forces many business schools to offer fast-track programs and degrees. For example, some schools are known for their MBA and other advanced business and management degree courses that are among the shortest in the nation, some lasting just a few weeks, thereby constituting even shorter duration for degree completion. Other schools have followed suit. With such an approach, degree completion time has become a very significant competitive factor. However, in the process some quality is no doubt lost, especially when educational leadership is not at its most effective and the quality of entrants into colleges and universities nationwide has declined dramatically and continues to be the case, as certain schools "dumb-down" programs and courses to cater to the "high-speed" candidate. This is not to say that there are not programs that have successfully maintained rigor and standards despite using time-frame as a competitive strategy. However, certain educational leadership at its essence seems to have a tradition closely related to mere time extension.

In the 21st century, the obstacles that business school educational leaders face are numerous, and these place great pressure on both the qualitative and quantitative aspects of teaching and learning, knowledge acquisition, storage, retrieval, and application. Professors must now balance their teaching time between course completion and ensuring full understanding and analyses of subject matters as well as providing scholarship. The time allowed for creative thinking and exploration becomes strained in this process and can affect the quality of education. Effective educational leadership in 21st century business schools is a collaborative process, where administrators and professors work cooperatively to foster high quality while ensuring that instruction matches the needs and requirements of the business world.

Imperatives for Business Leaders

Business schools are premier business places where business leaders lead and are created. The dean is the chief business leader in the 21st century business school, and his/her deputies sometimes include one or several associate and assistant deans, and expanding further to include directors and department chairs. The dean is the chief financial officer of the business school despite sometimes not directly being the one with that title in name. Many business schools tend to have associate or assistant deans of finance, or even directors of finance. Despite this, it is the responsibility first and foremost of the business school dean to market the school through his or her vision and strategic planning and networking. Business leadership in 21st century business schools tends to focus mostly on the non-educational processes and activities relevant for success. These include planning, finance, accounting, operations, marketing, and other key business functions.

As business leaders, 21st century business school deans and their associates are required to be market leaders and innovators, who understand the competitive nature of the business environment and the roles and functions of business schools in meeting the challenges of the environment and providing solutions to the many problems and issues. Business school leaders must recognize the need for effective and efficient as well as ethical management of organizational-institutional resources, high performance results, and profitability as part of delivering educational services and training successfully. The numbers and quality of graduates or prospective business leaders or entrepreneurs they produce must become a quantifiable measurement of success in an environment where there are many schools in the market offering business programs, often of the same types and contents. Managing the business school effectively and efficiently as well as ethically requires making proper, careful, and sound financial decisions. An ideal qualification for an effective business school dean or top administrative leader in the 21st century will therefore be sound financial education, perhaps an advanced degree in the areas of accounting and finance or other relevant fields, and extensive experience in the overall strategic management sector of business, especially the ability to balance and align at times competing stakeholder values and interests.

Business leaders must understand the importance of striking a balance among the relevant success factors and comprehending how the creation of value is best attained in the competitive environment. They must be able to network across educational and non-educational boundaries to bring to the forefront all the strategic imperatives that spell market leadership success. Business school deans, second-order administrators, and professors who are current and former business owners or managers and successful and experienced entrepreneurs, must impart their experiences and understanding of the real world to their students, also sharing these experiences and their knowledge with colleagues through interactive discussions. The business school of the 21st century has a "tough" job in creating knowledge workers with innovative ideas in a globally competitive world, where all the alternatives seem to have been discovered and applied already, and where all the inventions and innovations seem to have matured already. Many students will be led to think that there are no more new ideas, that we have exhausted the gamut of entrepreneurial creativity. Such individuals need *"eduvators,"* that is, educators who teach innovation. This is the role of business leaders in 21st century business schools: to foster creativity and innovation at all levels of the institution in order to spur new thoughts, inventions, ideas, service and product creations, and particularly the entrepreneurial spirit, and thereby create long-term, sustainable positive value for the student, the school, companies and organizations, communities, and society.

The Leadership Boundary

The business school dean of the 21st century must aspire to be an effective administrative leader, educational leader, and business leader. This is the ideal for successful business school leadership. The dean must be capable of leading fully in these three domains and even beyond. He or she must be a consummate businessperson, brilliant administrator, and knowledgeable educator. He or she must be an example and an exemplar of morality, ethics, and virtue. These values hold true for other administrators and key members of the business school. The roles and functions of administrative leadership, business leadership, and educational leadership are intimately interconnected and in most settings have no recognizable separation. However, in some business schools, administrative leadership is seen as the domain of the dean and associate and assistant deans; whereas educational leadership is seen as the domain of department chairs, program directors, and professors; and business leadership is seen as the domain of directors overseeing functional activities, such as budgeting, finance, operations, planning, marketing, public relations, among other defined functional activities specific to business schools according to their organizational structural models.

The 21st century business school is a highly transformative system since it must readily understand the nature of the environment in which it operates and recognize that the only viable system is one which changes along with the global system. Social responsibility and moral leadership are critical to balance stakeholders' needs and demands while making appropriate decisions that lead to organizational success and survival. When one examines the requirements of systems, leaders, and individuals, considering today's demands, one should recognize that business schools are essential tributaries to the complex world where knowledge and creativity are indispensable in a hyper-competitive environment. As such, the responsibilities of business school leaders span administrative, educational, and functional activities related to operations, as they work with a variety of individuals across these platforms to develop and maintain a competitive edge by sustaining and improving, as well as introducing, new programs, structures, and processes for survival and success.

Summary
The requirements for success in 21st century are enormous, and consequently demand that business school leaders recognize the importance of developing an adaptive, strong, and ethical mission and vision, the need for distinctiveness, effective leadership, morality, social responsibility and governance imperatives, training and development, and the value and rewards of becoming market leaders. With the demands for quality accredited programs, marketability, valuable and in-demand knowledge and skills, business schools must strive to deliver "above and beyond" markets and employers' expectations. Students in business schools should similarly expect the highest standards in instructions, technological knowledge, and to be equipped with the right skills and training that will allow them to survive and prosper as knowledge workers and future entrepreneurs. Modern leaders must develop their organizations as effective global response systems in an age when terror, natural disasters, market economics, and economic and political disruptions create new problems and challenges that demand innovative responses and effective solutions.

This book sought to raise and to address certain important and challenging issues confronting business schools today, including their role and function, leadership, accreditation, faculty research and scholarship, and faculty development and training. The authors have tried to provide some answers to at times difficult questions. They have in particular underscored the essential element of ethics to leadership, to business, and to the business student's education; they have presented and emphasized a conception of business as a profession; and they have provided a concrete example of a graduate level business ethics course. The authors also have attempted to supply some suggestions and recommendations in the areas of the training and development of faculty, particularly regarding online programs. The authors hope that their book has provided some guidance to the academic and business community in a useful and practical, as well as thoughtful and intellectually stimulating, manner; and they trust that they have advanced the discussion of these important issues, especially the moral imperative of ethics to leadership, business education, and business for the 21st century environment.

Bibliography

AACSB 2009 Accreditation standards changes and updates. *The Association to Advance Collegiate Schools of Business.* http://www.aacsb.edu/accreditation/standardsreport-revised23Jan09, retrieved June 28, 2009.

Alsop, Ronald (September 17, 2003). Right and Wrong: Can business schools teach students to be virtuous? *The Wall Street Journal, p. R9.*

Alsop, Ronald (July 11, 2006). M.B.A. Programs Blend Disciplines To Yield Big Picture. *The Wall Street Journal, p. B5.*

Alsop, Ron (September 18, 2007). Hass Takes New Tack on Investing: M.B.A. Students to Run Fund Focusing on Socially Responsible Firms. *The Wall Street Journal, p. B8.*

Alsop, Ron (June 19, 2007). Why Teaching of Ethics Continues to Be Lacking. *The Wall Street Journal, p. B7.*

Anders, George (September 26, 2007). Business Schools Forgetting Missions? *The Wall Street Journal, p. A2.*

Andreas School of Business. (2009). *AACSB International Accreditation.* Miami, Florida: Barry University. Retrieved August 6, 2009, from: http://www.barry.edu/business/about/aacsb.htm

Bateman, Joann Sandra (1998). Ethical Dilemma Survey of Undergraduate and Graduate Students. Doctoral Dissertation. The H. Wayne Huizenga School of Business and Entrepreneurship. Nova Southeastern University.

Bedeian, Arthur G. (2002). The Dean's Disease: How the Darker Side of Power Manifests Itself in the Office of the Dean. Academy *of Management Learning and Education, Vol. 1, No. 2, pp. 164-73.*

Bennis, W. G. and O'Toole, J. (2005). How business schools lost their way. *Harvard Business Review,* 83(5), pp. 96-105.

Bisoux, Tricia (July-August 2006). Flex-Time for the MBA. *BizEd, pp. 23-27.*

Bloodgood, James M., Tunley, William H., and Mudrack, Peter (October 2008). The Influence of Ethics Instruction, Religiosity, and Intelligence on Cheating Behavior. *Journal of Business Ethics, Vol. 82, No. 3, pp. 558-71.*

Brant, Martha and Ohtake, Miyoko (April 14, 2008). A Growth Industry: Business schools are teaching entrepreneurs how to get rich helping to save the environment. *Newsweek, p. 64.*

Bruner, Robert (August 20, 2009). Professor Says Business Schools and Students Can Take Away Lessons from Financial Crisis. *The Wall Street Journal, p. B5.*

Bebchuk, Lucian (2007). The Myth of the Shareholder Franchise. *Harvard Law School Program on Corporate Governance.* Retrieved May 10, 2007 from: http://www.law.harvard.edu/programs/olin-cener/corporate-governance.

Buell, Kevin E. (2009). The Relationship of Ethics Education to the Moral Development of Accounting Students. Doctoral Dissertation. The H. Wayne Huizenga School of Business Administration. Nova Southeastern University.

Cavico, F. J. and Mujtaba, B. G. (January 2010). An assessment of business school's student retention, accreditation, and faculty scholarship challenges. *Contemporary Issues in Education Research,* 3(1), pp. 01-13 (in press).

Cavico, F. J. and Mujtaba, B. G. (2009). *Business Ethics: The Moral Foundation of Leadership, Management, and Entrepreneurship (2nd edition).* Pearson Custom Publications. Boston, United States.

Cavico, F. J. and Mujtaba, B. G. (2009). The State of Business Schools, Business Education, and Business Ethics. *Journal of Academic and Business Ethics,* 2, 1-18. Available at: http://www.aabri.com/manuscripts/09300.pdf

Degrees Conferred by School Academic Year 2007-2008. (2009). *Registrar's Office, Harvard University.* Boston, MA: Harvard University. Retrieved July 28, 2009, from: http://www.provost.harvard.edu/institutional_research/FB2008_09_Completions.pdf

Degrees Conferred by Program: Academic Year 2007-2008. (2009). *Registrar's Office, Harvard University.* Boston, MA: Harvard University. Retrieved July 28, 2009, from: http://www.provost.harvard.edu/institutional_research/FB2008_09_Completions.pdf

Derrick, M. Gail and Carr, Paul B. (December 2008). Global Learning and Education for the 21st Century. *HRM Review, pp.16-19.*

Dizik, Alina (April 15, 2009). A Business School Learns to Specialize. *The Wall Street Journal, p. D4.*

Dvorak, Phred (February 12, 2007). M.B.A. Programs Hone "Soft Skills." *The Wall Street Journal, p. B3.*

Engardio, Pete (January 27, 2007). Beyond the Green Corporation. *Business Week, Special Report, pp. 50-64.*

Fox, Adrienne (August, 2007). Corporate Responsibility Pays Off. *HR Magazine, pp.43-47.*

Ghoshal, S. (2005). Bad management theories are destroying good management practices. *Academy of Management Learning and Education,* (4(1), pp. 75-91.

Glader, Paul (June 22, 2009). The Jack Welch MBA Coming to Web. *The Wall Street Journal, B1, B2.*

Gloecker, Geoff (November 16, 2009). A Brutal Wakeup Call. *Business Week,* pp.48-56.

Green, Hardy (November 5, 2007). Are B-Schools a Blight on the Land? *Business Week, p. 90.*

Heron, W. Thomas (2006). An Examination of the Moral Development and Ethical Decision-making of Information Technology Professionals. Doctoral Dissertation. The H. Wayne Huizenga School of Business and Entrepreneurship. Nova Southeastern University.

Hickman, Melissa S. (2008). Religiosity and Ethical Reasoning in Accounting Students. Doctoral Dissertation. The H. Wayne Huizenga School of Business and Entrepreneurship. Nova Southeastern University.

Huang, Chunlong (2006). Cross-Cultural Ethics: A Study of Cognitive Moral Development and Moral Maturity of U.S. and Japanese Expatriate Managers in Taiwan and Taiwanese Managers. Doctoral Dissertation. The H. Wayne Huizenga School of Business and Entrepreneurship. Nova Southeastern University.

Jacobs, M. (April 24, 2009). How business schools have failed business. *The Wall Street Journal, p. A13.*

Karlgaard, Rich (February 16, 2009). Failure of Morality, Not Capitalism. *Forbes, p. 21.*

Locke, Michelle (September 25, 2007). Balancing profit, planet. *The Miami Herald, p. 4C.*

Maidment, Fred, Coleman, John, and Barzan, Stan (2009). Characteristics of Executive MBA Programs at Public Colleges in the United States. *Research in Higher Education Journal, Volume 4, pp. 1-9.*

McFarlane, D.A. (2008). Effectively Managing the 21st Century Knowledge Worker. *Journal of Knowledge Management Practice, Vol. 9, No. 1*, March 2008; Retrieved August 3, 2009, from: http://www.tlainc.com/articl150.htm

McFarlane, D.A. (2008). Toward A Knowledge Management Body of Knowledge (KMBOK): A Philosophical Discourse in KM Concepts and Ideas. *Journal of Knowledge Management Practice, Vol. 9, No. 4*, December 2008. Retrieved August 5, 2009, from: http://www.tlainc.com/articl167.htm

Merritt, Jennifer (September 16, 2002). For MBAs, Soul-Searching 101: Now, B-schools are emphasizing ethics and responsibility. *Business Week, p. 64.*

Merritt, Jennifer (October 18, 2004). Welcome to Ethics 101: B-schools are trying a host of new methods to teach MBAs lasting lessons in leadership principles. *Business Week, p.90.*

Merritt, Jennifer (January 27, 2003). Why Ethics Is Also B-School Business. *Business Week, p. 105.*

Mitroff, I. I. (2004). An open letter to the deans and faculties of American business schools. *Journal of Business Ethics*, 54, pp. 185-189.

Mujtaba, B. G. (2010). *Workplace Diversity Management: Challenges, Competencies and Strategies (2nd edition).* ILEAD Academy Publications; Davie, Florida, United States.

Mujtaba, B. G. (2010). *Business ethics of retail employees: How ethical are modern workers?* ILEAD Academy Publications; Davie, Florida, United States.

Mujtaba, B. G. (1996). Business Ethics Survey of Supermarket Managers and Employees. UMI Dissertation Service. A Bell & Howell Company. UMI Number: 9717687.

Mujtaba, B. G. and McCartney, T. (2010). *Managing Workplace Stress and Conflict amid Change, 2nd edition*. ILEAD Academy Publications; Davie, Florida, United States.

Mujtaba, B. G., Cavico, Frank J., McCartney, Timothy O., and DiPaolo, Peter T. (May/June 2009). Ethics and Retail Management Professionals: An Examination of Age, Education, and Experience Variables. *American Journal of Business Education, Vol. 2, No.3, pp. 13-25.*

Mujtaba, B.G. and Sims, R.L. (2006). Socializing Retail Employees in Ethical Values: The Effectiveness of the Formal versus Informal Methods. *Journal of Business and Psychology,* 21(2), 261-272. Available at: http://www.springerlink.com/content/18r533570827151h/

Mujtaba, B. G. and Preziosi, R. C. (2006). *Adult Education in Academia: Recruiting and Retaining Extraordinary Facilitators of learning.* 2nd Edition. ISBN: 1593114753. Information Age Publishing. Greenwich, Connecticut.

Neubaum, D. O., Pagell, M., Drexler Jr., J. A., McKee-Ryan, F. M., and Larson, E. (2009). Business Education and Its Relationship to Student Personal Moral Philosophies and Attitudes Toward Profits: An Empirical Response to Critics. *Academy of Management Learning and Education,* 8(1), pp. 9-24.

Nonis, S. and Swift, C.O. (2001). An Examination of the Relationship between Academic Dishonesty and Workplace Dishonesty: A Multicampus Investigation. *Journal of Business Ethics,* 77(2), pp. 69-76.

Owen, Robert S. (February 2009). Managing a U.S. Business School Professor Shortage. *Research in Higher Education Journal, Volume 2, pp. 1-10.*

Sauser, William I. (2008). Regulating Ethics in Business: Review and Recommendations. *SAM Management in Practice, Volume 12, Number 4, pp.2-7.*

Schmalensee, Richard (November 27, 2006). Where's the 'B' in B-Schools? *Business Week, p. 118.*

Solberg, J., Strong, C.K., and McQuire, C., Jr. (1995). Living (not learning) ethics. *Journal of Business Ethics, Vol. 14, pp. 71-81.*

Snyder, R. L., Kizer, L. E., Mujtaba, B. G., and Khanfar, N. M. (July 2009). Comparing and Managing the Relative Importance and Ranking of Reasons for Selecting the Masters' of Business Administration Program. *American Journal of Business Education (AJBE), 2(4), 55-63.*

Trapnell, Jerry E. (November 07, 2009). AACSB International: A Focus on Faculty. Keynote Presentation at the *Academy of Business Disciplines*, 11th Annual Meeting, Ft. Myers Beach, Florida.

Trends in bachelor's degrees conferred by degree-granting institutions in selected fields of study: 1996–97, 2001–02, and 2006–07. U.S. Department of Education, National Center for Education Statistics. (2009). *Digest of Education Statistics*, 2008 (NCES 2009-020). Retrieved July 28, 2009, from: http://nces.ed.gov/programs/digest/d08/figures/fig_15.asp

U.S. Department of Education, National Center for Education Statistics. (2009). *Digest of Education Statistics*, 2008 (NCES 2009-020), Chapter 3. Retrieved July 28, 2009, from http://nces.ed.gov/FastFacts/display.asp?id=37.

Winfield, Nicole (July 8, 2009). Pope calls for ethics in finance. *The Miami Herald, p. 11A.*

Wolfe, A. (May-June 1993). We've had enough business ethics. *Business Horizons, pp. 1-3.*

Workplace Visions (2007). Social Responsibility and HR Strategy. *Society for Human Resource Management, No. 2, pp. 2-8.*

Zakaria, Fareed (June 22, 2009). Greed is Good (To A Point). N*ewsweek, pp. 41-45.*

Index

A

AACSB · 2, 20, 30, 31, 32, 33, 34, 35, 37, 38, 39, 42, 117, 123
academic dean · 57
Academic leadership · 52
academically qualified · 32, 34
ACBSP · 20
accounting · 27, 86, 94, 118, 119
actively participating · 32, 34, 37, 38, 43
actual learning · 102
Adults are *autonomous* · 99
America · 1, 2
American workers · 3
architecture · 94
Articles of Incorporation · 79
Assessment · 102, 109, 110
asynchronously · 101, 102, 103

B

Bateman · 59, 60, 123
Bazan · 38
Bedeian, A. · 50
Benedict XVI · 95
Bennis · 2, 123
Bentham · 63
Bernie Madoff · 3
blended · 97, 108
Bloodgood · 57, 124
bottom-line · 1, 28, 54
breakout · 47
Buell · 59, 124
Building trust · 50
Busch Gardens · 111
Business Consulting · 29
Business Ethics · 29, 57, 124, 126, 127
Business Management Code of Ethics · 95
Business managers · 66, 95
Business school deans · 119

C

Carr · 60, 125
carrot · 42
Categorical Imperative · 63

Cavico · 1, 2, 61, 124, 127
Cavico, Frank · 134
chairship · 114
charity day · 77
Charity in Truth · 96
chat sessions · 104
China · 6
Civil Rights Act · 62
cluster sites · 43, 44
cohort · 45
Coleman · 38, 126
Collaborative efforts · 42
Commercial speech · 81
Communication · 49
Compensate · 102
competitive edge · 12, 29, 115, 121
Constitution · 81
copyright · 2
Corporate actions · 82
corporate entity · 79
corporate governance · 3, 71, 78, 79, 81, 86, 88, 89, 90, 92, 95
Corporate managers · 78
corporate obligations · 80
corporate social responsibility · 66, 78
Corporations act · 82
Corporations possess · 82
Craft and tradespersons · 94
Critical components · 49
cyberspace technologies · 98, 106

D

deanship · 114, 115, 116
Department of Education · 6, 7, 128
Derrick · 60, 125
Developing and educating faculty · 98
directorship · 114
Discussion Boards · 104
Disney World · 111
distance education · 97, 98, 100, 111, 112
Distance education · 98, 112
Drexler · 1, 127
Drucker · 98
due process · 81

Author Biographies

Dr. Frank J. Cavico is a professor of Business Law and Ethics at the H. Wayne Huizenga School of Business and Entrepreneurship of Nova Southeastern University. He serves as Lead Professor for the graduate course, The Values of Legality, Morality, and Social Responsibility in Business. In 2000, he was awarded the Excellence in Teaching Award by the Huizenga School. In 2006, he was honored as Professor of the Year by the Huizenga School. Professor Cavico holds a J.D. degree from St. Mary's University School of Law and a B.A. from Gettysburg College. He also possesses a Master of Laws degree from the University of San Diego School of Law and a Master's degree in Political Science from Drew University. Professor Cavico is licensed to practice law in the states of Florida and Texas. He has worked as a federal government regulatory attorney and as counsel for a labor union; and has practiced general civil law and immigration law in South Florida. He is author of four books on law and ethics with his Huizenga School colleague, Dr. Bahaudin Mujtaba, as well as the author of several law review and journal articles.

Dr. Bahaudin G. Mujtaba is Department Chair and an Associate Professor of Management and Human Resources at Nova Southeastern University's H. Wayne Huizenga School of Business and Entrepreneurship. Bahaudin has served as manager, trainer, and management development specialist in the corporate arena as well as a director, department chair, and faculty member in academia. His areas of research are ethics, higher education assessment, leadership, training, and diversity management. Dr. Mujtaba is the author of several books on diversity, leadership, mentoring, change management, cross cultural management, and international, ethical, and legal challenges. He is the founder of the International Leadership Education and Associate Development Academy (ILEAD Academy, LLC), which is a consulting and publishing organization that serves clients with their training and Print-On-Demand (POD) book publication needs.

Dr. Donovan A. McFarlane is the founder of THE DONOVAN SOCIETY LLC. Donovan earned an M.B.A. as well as B.S. in Business Administration from the H. Wayne Huizenga School of Business and Entrepreneurship, Nova Southeastern University, and M.I.B. degree and Graduate Certificate in International Business from St. Thomas University. He also earned an M.B.A. in Human Resources Management from Frederick Taylor University, M.B.A. from Barrington University, D.B.A. from California Pacific University, B.S., M.S., Ph.D. from American Institute of Holistic Theology, Msc.D., M.Msc., B.Msc. from University of Metaphysics, Mpsy.D. from the University of Sedona, and M.R.S. from NationsUniversity. Published in both academic peer-reviewed and professional journals, Dr. McFarlane is a member of the International Honor Society for Business Management and Administration, the National Catholic College Honor Society, and National Honor Scholars Society. He has worked for several years as an Adjunct Professor in Business and served as Reviewer for the Society for Marketing Advances Dissertation Proposal Competition and Advisory Director for the Franklin Publishing Company.

Principle, particularly moral principle, can never be a weathervane, spinning around this way and that with the shifting winds of expediency. Moral principle is a compass forever fixed and forever true. And that is as important in business as it is in the classroom.

Edward R. Lyman

The most important human endeavor is the striving for morality in our actions. Our inner balance and even our very existence depend on it. Only morality in our actions can give beauty and dignity to life.

Charles Dickens

Ethics, too, are nothing but reverence for life. That is what gives me the fundamental principle of morality, namely, that good consists in maintaining, promoting, and enhancing life, and that destroying, injuring, and limiting life are evil.

Albert Schweitzer

The Value of Moral Education

While we teach and impart knowledge to create,
As we stress in our globally competitive times the need to innovate,
Let us not forget the true purpose with which we educate:

To develop moral and ethical men and women to recover and renovate,
Our good to sustain and for our failures to compensate,
And to make for each pupil ourselves teachers to emulate!

This is the categorical imperative that we must all understand,
Whether by virtue of values or the Law of the Land:

That morality is more than an arbitrary command;
It is a human responsibility defining the core of a man,
It is the door to great leadership and key to any successful plan!

Donovan A. McFarlane

www.ingramcontent.com/pod-product-compliance
Lightning Source LLC
Chambersburg PA
CBHW031943190326
41519CB00007B/634